Samuel Curtis Upham

Notes from Sunland, on the Manatee River, Gulf Coast South Florida

Its Climate, Soil, and Productions

Samuel Curtis Upham

Notes from Sunland, on the Manatee River, Gulf Coast South Florida
Its Climate, Soil, and Productions

ISBN/EAN: 9783744746434

Printed in Europe, USA, Canada, Australia, Japan

Cover: Foto ©Andreas Hilbeck / pixelio.de

More available books at **www.hansebooks.com**

NOTES FROM

SUNLAND,

ON THE

Manatee River, Gulf Coast

OF

SOUTH FLORIDA.

ITS CLIMATE, SOIL AND PRODUCTIONS.

The Land of the Orange and Guava,
The Pine-Apple, Date and Cassava.

By SAMUEL C. UPHAM.

ILLUSTRATED.

BRAIDENTOWN, FLA.:
PHILADELPHIA, 25 SOUTH EIGHTH STREET.
PUBLISHED BY THE AUTHOR.
1881.

From a photograph by F. PINARD, Manatee and Tampa.

MADAM JULIA ATZEROTH,

The lady who raised the first coffee grown in the United States.

TO

HAMILTON DISSTON,

Treasurer of the

ATLANTIC AND GULF COAST CANAL

and

OKEECHOBEE LAND COMPANY,

Not because he is a millionaire, but for the interest he has evinced in the welfare and progress of Florida; for his integrity as a citizen, and his sterling worth as a man, this *Brochure* is respectfully dedicated by

THE AUTHOR.

PREFACE.

Two or three letters written by myself to friends at the North having found their way into print, I have been literally flooded with letters during the past six months, from all sections of the Union and British Provinces, asking for information in relation to the Manatee region of Florida. Hundreds have been replied to, and many remain unanswered for want of time. This little book has been written with the belief that it will answer the requirements of my numerous correspondents, and also prove a welcome guest to others who desire reliable information concerning this portion of the Gulf coast of South Florida. With these brief remarks I cast my little waif upon the tide of public opinion, with the hope that favorable breezes will waft it into the hands of those who will be benefited by its perusal.

SUNNYSIDE COTTAGE,
Braidentown, Florida, April 1, 1881.

CHAPTER I.

Manatee Bay—Its Tropical Scenery—Egmont Key—
Snead's Island—Date, Palm and Olive Trees—
Climate—Insects—Braidentown and its Surround-
ings—Manatee, the Oldest Town on the Bay—Its
Early History — Braiden Castle — Fair Oaks—
Orange Groves—Willemsenburg and Fogartyville.

The Manatee River, or, more properly speaking, bay, is one of the most picturesque sheets of
water in Florida. It is fourteen miles in length,
with an average width of one and a half miles.
One of its tributaries—the Manatee River proper
—extends still further eastward, some twenty
miles; and another northward, half that distance.
Its course is nearly due west to Egmont Key,
where it mingles its waters with those of Tampa
Bay and the Gulf of Mexico. It lies between the
twenty-seventh and twenty-eighth parallels of
north latitude, and in longitude $5\frac{1}{2}°$ west from
Washington. A person passing up the bay on the
mail steamer for the first time, will be charmed
with the tropical and semi-tropical scenery that
meets his view on either side of the bay, from its
mouth to Braidentown, the present terminus of
steamboat navigation. Egmont Key, with its

7

forest of cabbage palmettos nodding their evergreen plumes in the morning sun ; the stately date-
palms and olive trees on Snead's Island, on the
north side of the bay, and the pretty villas surrounded by young orange and banana groves on
the south side, between Palmasola city and Manatee, form a landscape of rare tropical beauty,
unexceled in the land of flowers, and unrivaled
by the fairest scenes in Italia's famed land.

Until quite recently, this part of Florida, the
great sanitarium of the world, has, comparatively
speaking, been a sealed book to the invalids and
pleasure-seekers of the North and West, who spend
their winters in Jacksonville, St. Augustine and
the towns on the St. Johns, Halifax and Indian
Rivers, and console themselves with the idea that
they have seen all parts of Florida worth visiting.
The principal drawback which the Gulf coast has
had to contend with, and which partially exists at
this time, is lack of speedy transportation and
comfortable hotel accommodations. These are
being remedied, and, when the Manatee region
shall have become as thickly populated as the St.
Johns, our facilities for transportation, etc., will
equal those of the Atlantic coast.

The railroad now being built by Eastern capi-
talists, between Palatka on the St. Johns and
Tampa at the head of the bay of that name on
the Gulf coast, will be completed within two years.

Then the iron horse, with bowels of fire, muscles of steel and breath of steam, with a shriek and a snort, will rush over the metallic track and annihilate time and space so rapidly, that the Atlantic and Gulf coasts will be within a few hours of each other. A narrow-gauge railroad from Tampa to the Manatee, and thence to Sarasota Bay, will soon follow, giving us direct and rapid communication with the principal cities of the North and West. The round-about route over King David's Transit Railroad to Cedar Key, and thence by steamboat to the Manatee, will then be abandoned, and henceforth remembered only as a necessity of by-gone days. The recent completion of the Louisville, Nashville and Great Southern Railroad, with a terminus at Pensacola, will soon give us direct and speedy communication with the cities of Louisville, Nashville, Cincinnati, Indianapolis, Chicago and St. Louis, and open up the best and most available markets for the fruits and vegetables of the Gulf coast. General Alexander, Vice-President of this company, recently expressed his willingness to assist in the establishment of a line of steamers between Pensacola and Manatee, touching at other points along the coast.

Our climate is far superior to that of any other part of Florida; and, I do not think I hazard much in saying, to that of any part of the habitable globe. Having, during a somewhat eventful life of sixty-two years, visited Europe, Asia, Africa, South and Central America, Mexico and California, I say, and "I say it boldly," that in my varied travels, nowhere have I found so healthful and desirable a climate as "Sunland," on the Manatee Bay. We are exempt from ice and the chilling blasts that sweep along the St. Johns and Halifax, and also from tornadoes and hurricanes, so destructive on the Atlantic coast.

Insects are neither numerous nor troublesome. I have been worse annoyed by mosquitoes in the City of Philadelphia than in this part of Florida. The ubiquitous flea is, I admit, rather prevalent here, but one soon becomes reconciled to his habits, and honors his drafts whenever he presents his bill. Snakes are not as numerous here as in Pennsylvania. There are, however, rattlesnakes and moccasins in Florida. The former I have never seen, and the latter but seldom. Those that came under my observation, appeared to be worse frightened than I was, and made a hasty exit. Alligators are not numerous in this section, and are comparatively harmless. Like a once noted statesman, they desire to be let alone. If closely cornered, they will fight; but they prefer to run, if a chance is offered for escape.

Braidentown, the embryo town of the Manatee, is situated on the south side of the bay, about eight miles above its entrance into Tampa Bay.

Located on a bluff some fifteen feet above tide-water, it commands a fine view of the surrounding country and of the entire bay. Being constantly fanned by the breezes from the gulf "with healing on their wings," it is in point of healthfulness all that the most fastidious pleasure-seeker or invalid could wish for. From Jack's Creek, its eastern boundary, to its western terminus, Ware's Creek, it contains a frontage on the bay of three-fourths of a mile, dotted with picturesque villas, surrounded by tropical fruits and flowers. Although yet in a chrysalis state, being scarcely two years old, it contains two boarding-houses, two stores, a meat-shop, post-office and a warehouse, with a wharf connecting it with the shore—the only one on the bay east of Palmasola city. Passengers for Manatee and other places on the bay are conveyed on shore in sail or row-boats. Major W. I. Turner, the projector of Braidentown, a Virginian by birth, has been a resident of Florida for forty-five years. Although on the shady side of life, he is still hale and hearty. May he live to see his bantling, now in her leading-strings, the county-seat of Manatee County. Stranger events have happened. This is an age of progress; the world moves, and Florida, after her Rip Van Winkle sleep of three hundred years, is moving with it.

Sportsmen visiting this place can be accommodated with sail·boats for fishing, or mule and ox teams for a hunting trip to the Miakka, the sportsman's paradise.   Captain Charles Miller and Billy Stowell, *alias* "Buffalo Bill," both "old salts" and reliable men, can be engaged with their respective crafts, the *Sancho Panza* and *Onkechi,* at reasonable rates.   Ox and mule teams can be had of John N. Harris and Dr. S. J. Tyler.

The reader will pardon a slight digression, and allow me to state, that if any person who knows how to run a hotel, will start one in Braidentown, he will most assuredly put money in his purse, and at the same time satisfy a great public want.   A hotel containing one hundred rooms, properly conducted, would be filled with guests six months of the year.   We have fish, oysters, clams and game in abundance, on which boarders could fare sumptuously every day.   Shall we have a hotel?

One and a half miles east of Braidentown, on the low, sandy beach of the bay, is the irregularly constructed village of Manatee.   A stranger visiting Manatee will invariably ask himself why a town was ever built here?   The following will solve the problem.   Adjacent to the village, in a southerly direction, are rich hammock lands, which, in consequence of their malarial surroundings, could not be domiciled by their owners. The pine land on the bay shore offering a more healthful location for building, the early settlers availed themselves of it and erected their log and palmetto cabins first, and afterward more pretentious and architectural structures. The Indian war breaking out soon after the first settlers had located at Manatee, their cabins formed the nucleus of a settlement as a protection against the savages. Thus Manatee became a village, and for many years was the only settlement on the Manatee Bay. The hospitality of her citizens is proverbial. The stranger within their gates who asks for bread is never requested to masticate a stone. Unfortunately, the citizens of Manatee are not as progressive as hospitable. A plank wharf or footway, connecting the steamboat warehouse with the shore, is badly needed, and should be constructed at once. There is a great deal of vitality lying dormant in the old town, which, if thoroughly aroused and properly applied, would place an entirely different aspect on the face of affairs. The village contains a Methodist church, five stores, three boarding-houses, a drug store, an academy, a meat-shop and a post-office. Dr. George Casper, an enterprising Manatcean, wishing to extend his usefulness, and being impressed with the belief that it would be a good thing to mix literature with physic, has issued the prospectus of a weekly newspaper, to be called the *Manatee County News.* It will be the pioneer paper of the county, and its editor will have plenty of elbow-room—Manatee

County being as large as the States of Connecticut and Rhode Island.

One mile east of Manatee, on a point of land formed by the junction of Braiden Creek with the bay, stands a historic structure, known as Braiden Castle. It is composed of a concrete of lime and oyster-shells, two stories high, surmounted by a cupola or observatory, constructed of wood, from which a charming view of the surrounding country can be had. South-east, Braiden Creek, winding like a silver thread among innumerable evergreen islands, presents a view worthy of a poet's dream. Westward, as far as the eye can scan, can be traced the blue waters of the bay glinting in the sun or dancing in the moonbeams on their way to the gulf. Northward, across the bay, the eye meets hammock, pine land and prairie stretching far away toward Tampa Bay. This old relic, scarred by Indian bullets, stands a sad memento of better days. Who shall write its history?

At Fair Oaks, about one and a half miles south of the castle, on a portion of the old Braiden plantation, is the largest and most thrifty young orange grove on the gulf coast of South Florida. It comprises nearly four thousand trees; belongs to the Hon. Charles H. Foster, ex-State Treasurer, and is a living, growing, bearing monument to Yankee pluck, enterprise and industry. Mr. Foster is now erecting at Fair Oaks the handsomest private residence in South Florida. The most direct route to Fair Oaks is by the way of Manatee, and the scenery *en route* is unsurpassed in the land of the myrtle and ivy. Leaving Rocky Ford, you pass Glen Falls, whose pellucid waters sparkle and dance over rock and through chasm, on their course to the Manatee. Graceful palms, with their evergreen foliage; stately live oaks, draped with pendant moss, swaying to and fro in the breeze; girdled oaks, gayly festooned from base to apex with ivy, yellow jessamine and Virginia creeper, gladden the eye on either side of the road, and orange-blossoms perfume the air with their delightful fragrance, rendering the scene enchanting as fairy land.

In the village of Manatee and adjacent hammock may be seen the orange groves of Mrs. Gates, Revs. Edmund Lee, A. A. Robinson and E. Glazier, Messrs. Pelote, Curry, Harllee, Mitchell, Vanderipe, Lloyd, Clark, Warner, McNeill, Casper, Gates, Wyatt, Adams, Broberg, Reed and Wilson. Mrs. Gates, Parson Lee and Major Adams also have banana groves in bearing. The latter gentleman is engaged in erecting a large concrete mansion, with carriage-house and servants' quarters of the same material. Situated in an eligible position on the bank of the bay, surrounded by tropical fruits, flowers and vines, whose evergreen foliage constantly waving in the breeze, renders the location highly picturesque.

Some four or five miles south of Manatee, *en route* to Sarasota Bay, are thrifty young orange groves, belonging to the Messrs. Helm, father and sons, Dryman, Marshall, Younglove, Dunham, Saunders, Azlin, Howell, Thompson, Williams and Whitted; and on Black-Jack Ridge, near Braidentown, may be seen the thrifty grove of Judge E. M. Graham. The groves of the Messrs. Helm are pronounced by every one who have seen them to be the most promising of their age in the State. They are only four years old, but will put to the blush many groves twice their age. They are monuments of clean and persistent culture.

On the west side of Ware's Creek, skirting the bay, is Willemsenburg, consisting of three houses and the frame of a mammoth hotel. This grim skeleton, gray with age, has a history. Erected originally by Dr. Hunter, at one time a noted physician of New York, and Charles W. Skinner, a Boston capitalist, on Sanibel, or "Sanitarium" Island, near Punta Rassa, it was soon blown or washed down. A portion of the wreck, with additional lumber from Cedar Key, was soon afterward erected at Sarasota Bay, where another partner, Dr. Dunham, of St. Louis, joined in the enterprise. A misunderstanding between the trio resulted in the withdrawal of the two medical men before the structure was completed. Mr. Skinner subsequently razed the building to the ground,

rafted it through Palmasola Bay into the Manatee, and erected it on its present site, where it has stood in an unfinished condition during the past five years. The decease of Mr. Skinner soon after its erection, caused its progress to stop as suddenly as did "my grandfather's clock" at the death of its owner.

Westward, separated by an imaginary line, is Fogartyville, a community composed principally of boat-builders and seafaring men, with their families. It contains a store, boat-builder's shed, half a dozen dwelling-houses, a floating dry-dock with two sections in working order, and two additional sections nearly completed. The Messrs. Fogarty and Captain Bhart are the owners of the dry-dock.

In this cozy little settlement, close down by the waters of the bay, lives Madam Julia Atzeroth, and in the garden attached to her house was cultivated with her own hands *the first coffee grown in the United States*. Madam Atzeroth, or Madam "Joe," as she is called by her friends, is a character, and deserves an extended notice.

CHAPTER II.

MADAM ATZEROTH—BIRTH, PARENTAGE AND MARRIAGE
—ARRIVAL IN NEW YORK—VISIT TO PHILADELPHIA,
EASTON AND NEW ORLEANS—ARRIVAL IN FLORIDA—
LOCATES ON TERRACEIA ISLAND—VICISSITUDES OF PIO-
NEER LIFE—A FRIEND IN NEED, A FRIEND INDEED—
ARRIVAL OF HER SISTER AND FAMILY—TRIP TO NEW-
NANSVILLE—CORN-DODGERS AND SAWDUST—DEATH OF
MRS. NICHOLS—REMOVAL TO FORT BROOKE, TAMPA—
COL. W. W. BELKNAP AND FAMILY—RETURN TO TER-
RACEIA—HOMESTEAD PAPERS ILLEGALLY EXECUTED—
RETURN AGAIN TO TAMPA—GALE OF 1846—REMOVE TO
PALMETTO—INDIAN WAR—SCENES DURING THE WAR OF
THE REBELLION—SELL OUT AT PALMETTO AND SETTLE
IN FOGARTYVILLE—FIRST COFFEE GROWN IN THE
UNITED STATES—ITS HISTORY.

MADAM JULIA ATZEROTH, whose maiden name
was Hunt, was born in the City of Bradford, near
the River Rhine, in Bavaria, on the 25th day of
December, 1807. Of a family of four children—
two males and two females—she is the only survi-
vor. The death of her mother occurring when
she was eleven years of age, she was adopted by
an uncle on the maternal side, with whom she
resided until she attained her majority. At the
age of twenty-four years she married Joseph At-

zeroth, also a native of Bavaria. The young couple soon after the birth of their first child, a daughter, left the Fatherland and immigrated to America. They arrived in New York in the month of August, 1841, where they remained only a few months. In consequence of the failing health of Madam Atzeroth, they visited Philadelphia and Easton, Pa.; but deriving no benefit from change of location at the North, her physician advised her to go South. They accordingly went to New Orleans, where they remained about one year. Madam Atzeroth's health not improving, her attending physician, a German, proposed a trip to Florida. Laying in a supply of provisions and medicines, and accompanied by the physician, they engaged passage on board the schooner *Essex*, a tender for the United States troops stationed at Fort Brooke, Tampa, where they arrived in the spring of 1843.

Soon after landing at Tampa, Mr. Atzeroth commenced prospecting for a desirable place to locate. After looking about for two or three weeks, he concluded to homestead one hundred and sixty acres of land on Terraceia Island, and on the 12th day of April, 1843, accompanied by his wife, little daughter, the German physician and his dog Bonaparte, landed on the east side of the island about midway of Terraceia Bay. The hammock was so dense that the men were compelled to use their axes to clear a space on which to pitch their tent. The underbrush and vines were so thick, and the progress made by the men so slow, that Madam Joe seized an axe and assisted them. This was her first attempt at chopping and grubbing in Florida. Since that time she has become an expert at the business. When the tent was erected and dinner prepared, it was eaten with a keen relish. From that time forward Madam Joe felt new life and strength. Her torpid liver began to perform its normal functions, and she forthwith discharged the physician and destroyed his medicines. The doctor went to Key West, where he died soon afterward.

Having become weary of tent-life, Madam Joe proposed to her husband the erection of a palmetto hut. Mr. Joe, as the madam always called her husband, drove the stakes for the frame and gathered the palmetto fans or branches. The madam mounted the roof and thatched it; but her work was performed so badly that the first shower of rain deluged the interior, and its inmates sought refuge under the table. The hut was subsequently re-thatched, and three of its corners made fast to trees, which prevented the wind from blowing it down. Soon after the completion of the hut, their provisions ran short, and Mr. Joe started in a canoe for Tampa to replenish them. On his return, adverse winds blew his frail craft around

Shaw's Point into Palmasola Bay, and becoming bewildered, he landed at Sarasota instead of Terraccia. After being buffeted about by the wind and waves for more than a week, he finally reached home. During his absence, Madam Joe and her child had no companion save the dog Bonaparte. The panthers, wild hogs and owls made the nights hideous with their screams, growls and hootings. One night a raid was made by an owl on the chickens roosting on the trees overhanging the hut. Madam Joe seized an old musket of the Methodist persuasion, which usually went off at half-cock, with the intention of frightening away the "wild varmints," but it was unloaded. Never having loaded a musket, she was in a quandary whether to put in first the powder or the shot. Luckily, she put in the powder before the shot, and stepping to the door of the hut, discharged the musket into the tops of the trees. She put in too much powder, and like another gun we read about, it

"Bore wide the mark and kicked its owner over."

The owl escaped that time in consequence of being at the wrong end of the musket. It was subsequently killed by Mr. Joe, and peace reigned once more among the chickens. Madam Joe subsequently became an expert with both the shot-gun and rifle, and if reports are reliable, her unerring aim has caused more than one red-skin to make a

hasty exit to the "happy hunting-grounds." She
can also ride a horse astride or otherwise—seldom
otherwise—like a Camanche.

Becoming disgusted with their frail palmetto
hut, Madam and Mr. Joe felled the trees and commenced the erection of a log-pen house, consisting
of two rooms, with a wide passage running between
them. As there were no saw-mills in the country,
boards could not be had at any price. The roof
of the house was covered with split cedar planks,
and the interstices between the logs filled with
moss and clay. A chimney was improvised of
sticks plastered with mud. Subsequently, glazed
sash for the windows were imported from New
Orleans. Meanwhile the axe had not been idle.
The stately live oaks and graceful palms around
the house had been felled and burned, the land
grubbed, and a good-sized vegetable garden was
in successful cultivation. Fort Brooke, some thirty
miles distant, offering a good market for their
surplus produce, they hired a man with a boat to
transport and sell their vegetables. Although
bountiful crops rewarded their labor, they were
not entirely happy. Madam Joe was anxious that
her only sister, residing in New York, should
emigrate with her family to Florida. But how
was the matter to be accomplished without money?
Where there is a will, there is always a way to
accomplish things which at first sight seem to be

impossibilities. The matter was laid before Col.
W W. Belknap, the commander of Fort Brooke,
who cheerfully advanced the required funds, and
Mr. Joe left immediately in a schooner for New
York, *via* Key West. The voyage was long and
tedious, but it was accomplished, and in due
course of time, Mr. Joe returned safely with his
brother-in-law, wife and child.

Another trouble now presented itself. The
Armed Occupation Act having expired previous to
locating their land on Terraceia, they were compelled to go to the United States Land Office, at
Newnansville, one hundred and sixty miles distant,
to file the requisite papers. The country being
wild and sparsely settled, Mr. Joe and Mr. Nichols,
his brother-in-law, were compelled to pack their
provisions on their backs, which rendered their
journey wearisome and slow. On the third day
they reached a cabin, where they remained over
night. While at breakfast on the following morning, most of their provisions were stolen by some
thieving negroes. The theft not being discovered
until they stopped at mid-day to lunch, they were
in a sad plight. They pushed on as fast as possi-
ble, and late in the evening came to a cabin inhabited by very poor people. A scanty supper
was set before them, which they ate and retired for
the night. The breakfast-table on the following
morning was bountifully supplied with hog, hominy

and corn-dodgers. Mr. Nichols having never before seen a corn-dodger, took a large mouthful of
one, and then walking deliberately to the door,
spat it out. On resuming his seat at the table,
he requested Mr. Joe, in German, not to eat those
saw-dust cakes. Mr. Joe, knowing the difference
between saw-dust and corn-meal, continued to put
away the dodgers, to the great disgust of his brother-in-law, who finished his breakfast on hog and
hominy. They finally reached Newnansville,
transacted their business and returned safely home,
after an absence of about two weeks.

Soon after the return of her husband from Newnansville, Mrs. Nichols gave birth to a child. It
lived only two hours, and in less than one week
from its birth its mother followed the little angel
to

" The undiscovered country, from whose bourne
No traveler returns."

The surviving child, a little girl two years old, was
adopted by Madam Joe, who reared and educated
her. She is at this time the wife of Mr. William
O'Neil, who resides at Palmetto, on the north side
of the Manatee Bay.

The money borrowed from Colonel Belknap still
remained unpaid, which was a source of great trouble to Madam Joe. She had the inclination, but
not the means to cancel the debt. The colonel
proposed to send for his family at the North, and

install Madam Joe as housekeeper. The proposition was cheerfully acquiesced in ; and early in the year 1845, Madam Joe, accompanied by her husband, daughter and niece, went to Tampa and resided in the house of Colonel Belknap, at Fort Brooke. The Terraceia homestead was left in charge of Mr. Nichols and a hired man. The colonel's family at that time consisted of his wife, two daughters and a son. That son, General W. W. Belknap, at present, I believe, a resident of New York, made an honorable and enviable record during the war of the Rebellion, and was afterward Secretary of War during a part of President Grant's administration.

During the eight months Madam Joe resided with the family of Colonel Belknap, she frequently saw the wily chief, Billy Bowlegs, and other noted Seminoles, for whom, to use her own words, she "cooked many a meal." Close confinement caused a recurrence of her old disease—liver complaint—and she reluctantly left the hospitable house of Colonel Belknap for her homestead on Terraceia, where by constant out-door exercise, she soon regained her usual health. Even at the present day, Madam Joe's universal panacea is "the grubbing-hoe and elbow-grease." She practices what she preaches, and unlike the medical profession, takes her own medicine. Soon after the return of Madam Joe and family to Terraceia,

Mr. Nichols concluded to go to New Orleans. During that year—1846—the yellow fever nearly depopulated the city, and Mr. Nichols was probably one of its victims, as he has never been heard from by his friends since he left Terraceia.

In the fall of 1846, one of the severest gales that ever visited this section of the country passed over Tampa, Terraceia, Palmetto and Manatee. Madam Joe's house was blown down and all her furniture destroyed. The hen-house was the only structure that survived the storm. The fowls were dispossessed of their domicile, and the family occupied it until another house was built.

In 1848, a government official visited this part of Florida to examine proofs of claimants to land under the Armed Occupation and Homestead Acts. On examining Madam Joe's papers, it was discovered that two permits had been issued for the same number. This error could only be rectified at the General Land Office in Washington. It was deemed advisable by Madam Joe and her husband to return to Tampa and remain there until the mistake in relation to their homestead could be rectified. Mr. Joe hired a man to assist him in building a house at Tampa, and they went up the Hillsborough River to cut logs and make shingles for the structure. In the month of September the logs for the house were formed into a raft and the shingles placed on it. Everything being in readiness for a start, a furious gale set in, which destroyed the raft and scattered the logs and shingles for miles along the banks of the river. Having gathered the logs and shingles together and rafted them down to Tampa, Mr. Joe visited his family at Terraceia, where he learned that during the late storm his wife, child and niece had taken refuge in the house of a friend on another part of the island. He returned to Tampa, and his family followed soon after. When Madam Joe arrived, she did not admire the location her husband had selected for the house. The frame was taken down and erected on a lot on the town-side of the river, and was soon occupied by the family. The property is still owned by Madam Joe.

Misfortunes, it is said, never come single-handed. In the early part of 1849, Mr. Joe injured one of his feet, and soon after was attacked with chills and fever, which, despite medical treatment, continued nine months. At this time Madam Joe's finances were at a fearfully low ebb; but being equal to the emergency, she cast about for something to do whereby she could earn an honest penny. She accordingly started a home-made beer and cake shop, which being liberally patronized by the soldiers, soon placed her in easy financial circumstances. Her husband at the same time kept a sutler's store at Fort Chiconicla.

About this time a partly-finished house, built by

a friend—Mr. Reece—in Palmetto, was sold by the sheriff, and Madam Joe became the purchaser, with the hope that Mr. Reece would be able to redeem the property. Failing to do so, Madam Joe and family left Tampa and located in Palmetto in the year 1851. Here they opened a small store, in which they did a thriving business. They also cultivated their farm on Terraceia Island, and by degrees, as their means permitted, stocked it with cattle, horses and hogs. Additions were also made to their stock of goods, and finally they purchased a colored man, who was an excellent farm hand, and proved of great service to his owners.

In 1855 another Indian war broke out. Volunteer companies, home-guards and boat companies were organized for protection against Indian incursions. Many plantations were abandoned and homes broken up. Mr. Joe belonged to one of the boat companies, and a ten days' scout being prolonged to twenty days, it was reported that the entire party had been massacred by the Indians. During the scout they visited the Indian camps in the Everglades, from whence Mr. Joe brought away as trophies a silver cup and a spoon belonging to Billy Bowlegs. The cup was subsequently sold to Colonel Jewett, U. S. A. The country was in a state of commotion and fever of excitement until the close of the war, in 1858. During these eventful years, Madam Joe stood guard with her musket or rifle whenever her services were required. She never showed the white feather.

Peace had scarcely been restored, when the civil war of 1861 broke out, and Florida was again in a state of anarchy. Mr. Joe enlisted in the Confederate service, and served in Tennessee and Kentucky. At the close of the war, Madam Joe sold her place at Palmetto, with the intention of returning to Europe, but her physician informed her that she could not survive a change of climate, which induced her to abandon the idea of visiting the Fatherland. The family again took up their residence on Terraceia, where Mr. Joe died on the 29th of October, 1871. Madam Joe sold part of her Terraceia plantation and moved to Fogartyville, her present location, in the year 1873. Her garden at this place comprises only four acres, but nowhere else in Florida can be found so many different varieties of trees, plants, vegetables, vines, shrubs and flowers. Mrs. William Fogarty, the daughter of Madam Joe, with her husband and son, reside with the madam. Here, in the year 1876, was planted a few grains of Mexican coffee, received from a neighbor, Mrs. E. S. Warner. On the 20th of February, 1880, Madam Joe sent to the Commissioner of Agriculture, at Washington, the *first pound of coffee grown in the United States*, for which she received ten dollars. This spring she has sent to the Agricultural Department, at Washington, four pounds of coffee, the product of two trees. Next year she will have eight coffee trees in bearing, and at least one hundred young trees in her nursery. As quite a diversity of opinion exists in relation to the origin of the seed from which the first coffee was grown in the United States, I append the following communications from Mrs. E. S. Warner, of Manatee, Fla., and Dr. A. A. Russell, of Cordova, Mexico, published in the Tampa *Tribune*, of September 26th, 1880:

"MANATEE, FLA., *August 30th, 1880.*

"DR. WALL: Dear Sir—I inclose a letter from Dr. A. A. Russell, of Cordova, Mexico, the gentleman from whose plantation the coffee-seed was procured that has been successfully reproduced by Madam Atzeroth here. As the subject of coffee-raising in this State is causing considerable inquiry, and as this letter contains much valuable information on the subject, I submit it to you for publication, asking the favor of having a copy forwarded to the doctor from your office as soon as issued. Very respectfully,

"E. S. WARNER."

"CORDOVA, MEXICO, *May 19th, 1880.*

"MRS. E. S. WARNER: Madam—It was quite a pleasure to receive your very kind letter of April 1st. I congratulate you most heartily, and am proud to learn that from the *seed I sent was produced the first coffee in the States.* I think I wrote you that the plant requires shade. In this climate we prefer to plant in fresh, timbered land; cutting out at first only the undergrowth, and taking out a few trees every year after for two or three years, thus graduating the shade and ventilating as appears to be required. The palatine (or plantain, or banana, as you probably call it) makes a good shade, and may be cut out, or under leaves trimmed off as may seem to be necessary. Coffee requires a rich, vegetable soil, or manure. The berry is fully ripe when dark red, but the grain is matured if the berry is picked when it has become yellow or only turning red; however, the coffee is of better quality if the berry is fully ripe, that is, of a deep or dark red. When gathered, it should be spread out at once to dry in the sun. It may be dried on mats, scaffolds or platforms of planks or boards. In good or favorable weather it requires about three weeks to dry. Here it is often dried on the ground. It may be spread from two to four inches thick, and should be stirred twice or three times a day; and if it should get wet a few times on the dryer, before half dry, no harm will be done and the coffee not injured in the least, if frequently stirred to prevent fermentation. When half dry it should be protected from rain and dew. If it has been wet a few times it will be more easily cleaned, but if frequently wet it will be of a darker color; also much darker, and even black and spoiled, if allowed to heat and ferment. It may be pulped by some of the pulping machines now in use, the day it is gathered, then washed and dried. The pulped coffee will dry in a few days, occupies less space in drying, and is of a lighter color, which, with you, I presume, are considerations of little importance at present.

"You will know the coffee is sufficiently dry when the hull crushes readily under the foot. The most simple, and, by the way, not a very bad process for cleaning the coffee, is the primitive mode of cleaning rice; that is, to beat it out in a deep mortar with a heavy pestle, and as the chaff accumulates dip out the coffee with a cup in the left hand, pour-

ing back into the mortar from the same height, at the same
time blowing off the chaff with a fan in the right hand, re-
peating the process until clean.

"There are a variety of machines for hulling and cleaning coffee, which will be a matter of consideration when the
production requires it. Now that you have succeeded in
producing the grain, you will have less difficulty in propa-
gating from the acclimated seed, which should be thoroughly
ripe, squeezed out of the pulp and dried in the shade. Hope
you will continue successfully, and establish plantations of
importance.   Your obedient servant,

"A. A. RUSSELL."

The portrait of Madam Joe, forming the *frontis-
piece* of this book, is a truthful likeness. Above
the medium height of her sex, with features bronzed
by a tropical sun and the exposure and hardships
of a pioneer life, she is nevertheless a well-preserved matron of seventy-four years, with as noble
and generous a heart as ever pulsated within the
breast of a human being. She is passionately fond
of music and waltzing, and can

"Trip the light fantastic toe"

as gracefully as a miss of sixteen. May her days
in the land be prolonged beyond fourscore years
and ten.

CHAPTER III.

The Warners, Mother and Sons—Palmasola City—
Steam Saw-mill and other Improvements — Sam
Nichols and his Shell-mound— Palmasola Bay—
Sarasota Bay and its Surroundings—Snead's Island
— Shell-mound—Date-palm and Olive Trees—
Uncle Joe and his Dogs with Glass Eyes—Sapp's
Point—Palmetto—The Patten and Turner Plan-
tations—Judah P. Benjamin—Oak Hill—Terra-
ceia Island—Landing of De Soto in 1539.

Westward of Fogartyville, on the south side
of the bay, among the most prominent residences,
are those of the Warners, mother and sons.
Thence westward, across a bayou, on a sand-spit
projecting into the bay, stands the steam saw and
planing-mill of Messrs. W. S. Warner & Co.,
just completed. This mill, wharf and warehouse
are the *nucleus* of Palmasola City, which is soon to
skirt the adjacent sand hills, and cause the surrounding "wilderness to blossom as the rose."
Mr. Warner is a Bay State Yankee of indomitable
pluck, and his partner, Mr. J. S. Beach, who resides at Terre Haute, Ind., controls the money
bags of a national bank. If capital and pluck
can build a city, the success of Palmasola may be

33

set down as assured. Along the bay, west of the Warners, are the ranches of Messrs. Sweetzer, Burgess, Sykes and Bishop. A few miles further west is Shaw's Point, at the mouth of the bay. Here, on an immense shell-mound, surrounded by hammock and pine land, Mr. Sam Nichols, a native of Alabama, has entered a homestead of 160 acres of land. Although severely wounded during our late "unpleasantness," Mr. Nichols has beaten his musket into a plowshare, his sword into a pruning-hook, and, like a good citizen, is earning his bread by the sweat of his brow.

Along the Gulf coast, southward, skirting Palmasola and Sarasota Bays, may be found the hospitable homes of Messrs. Farrar, Adams, Moore, Buckner, Harp, Stephonse, Tyler, Spang, Crowley, Dorch, Callan, Riggin, Dunham, Smith, Helveston, Whitaker, Willard, Bidwell, Edmondson, C. E. and M. R. Abb⬛Liddell, Greer, Yonge, Boardman, Young, ⬛ter, Conliff, Woodworth, Jones, Anderson⬛er, Hansen, Bronson Bros., Clower, Low⬛b, Griffith, Bacon, Knight, Guptrel and Roberts.

On the north side of Manatee Bay, at its entrance into Tampa Bay, is Snead's Island, separated from the mainland by a narrow and shallow "cut-off" leading into Terraceia Bay, and also by a wider and deeper channel opening into Tampa Bay, and separating it from Terraceia Island. Midway of the island, fronting on Manatee Bay, is a curiosity in the shape of a shell-mound or earth-work, crescent-shaped, and some forty feet in height. The distance between the points of the crescent on the bank of the bay, is five hundred feet. On the highest point of the mound, and nearly in the centre, stands a frame dwelling, somewhat dilapidated, erected by a former owner of the place. On the eastern angle are two date-palm and two olive trees. The former are fifteen inches in diameter and forty feet in height. The latter are eighteen inches in diameter two feet above the ground, and fifty feet in height. Both the olive and date-palms bear fruit; the former in large quantities. On the mound in the centre of the crescent, and near the house, are two olibanum trees, eighteen inches in diameter and fifty feet in height. Was this mound an Indian burial place, or was it thrown up by the early Spanish invaders as a defense against the Natchez, a warlike and semi-civilized tribe of Indians, who, at the time of the Spanish conquest, inhabited this part of Florida? *Quien sabe?*

The only human occupants of the island at this time are uncle Joe Franklin and his wife, an aged couple. Uncle Joe lives in a palmetto hut with a shell floor, and with the old 'oman and two glass-eyed dogs as companions,

"His hours in cheerful labor fly."

Uncle Joe is a character, and all visitors to the Manatee should call on him, examine his mammoth wild fig tree and hedge of century plants. *Mem.* Ask him to chain his dogs before you go ashore, otherwise the seat of your inexpressibles will require repairs. I have been there.

Eastward, above the Terraceia cut-off, is Sapp's Point. Further along, and directly opposite Braidentown, is Palmetto, a young town containing two stores and a post-office. The reader will perceive that Uncle Sam distributes post-offices in Florida with a lavish hand. We have three of these convenient institutions within a radius of one and a half miles—Braidentown, Manatee, Palmetto—and Palmasola City, only three miles distant, will have one as soon as Postmaster Warner shall build an office to protect the mail matter of that growing city.

Immediately in the rear of Palmetto is a prairie of several miles in extent. North-east of the town, about one mile distant in the hammock, Mr. Hendricks, of Palmetto, has a promising six-years-old orange grove, grown from seeds planted with his own hands. Mr. Hendricks cultivates vegetables between the rows of his orange trees, and last year he realized several hundred dollars by shipping his early tomatoes, cucumbers and snap-beans to New York and other Northern markets. To Mr. Hendricks belongs the credit of starting the early vegetable boom in the Manatee region. .

Mr. David Zehner, from Louisiana, has recently purchased a strip of scrub hammock, east of the town, where he intends to make the cultivation of grapes and strawberries a specialty. He has already received several thousand cuttings and plants of the choicest varieties. A few miles further eastward, you reach the plantation of Major W. I. Turner, the god-father of Braidentown, who has forty acres in tomatoes, cucumbers, squashes and beans. He has already commenced shipping his vegetables to the Northern markets.

Half a mile east of Major Turner's is the extensive plantation of Major George Patten. General Hiram W. Leffingwell, ex-United States Marshal for the Eastern District of Missouri, has recently purchased 200 acres of this land, and is negotiating for more. Two of the general's sons, with their families and an unmarried nephew, are now encamped on the land, and are busily engaged in erecting dwelling-houses and the necessary out-buildings. The general and his wife will arrive later in the season. In addition to the cultivation of the various fruits of the citrus family, the general will devote his attention to general farm crops and the growing of early vegetables for the Northern and Western markets. Another St. Louis gentleman, Mr. C. G. B.

Drummond, Assistant U. S. District Attorney, has purchased 120 acres of land on the Rogers' hammock near Oak Hill, on which he will set out an orange grove this summer.

Mr. H. O. Cannon, a California Argonaut, and late resident of New Albany, Ind., after having spent several winters prospecting Florida, has, like a sensible man, concluded to pitch his tent on the Patten plantation. With this view, he has purchased twenty acres of land, which he has commenced grubbing and fencing, preparatory to planting an orange and lemon grove. Mr. C. H. Walworth, of Milwaukee, has purchased twenty acres of land adjoining Mr. Cannon, which he will have cleared, grubbed and planted in orange and lemon trees this year.

In *ante bellum* times, the present Patten plantation was know first as the Gamble, and afterward as the Cofield and Davis plantation, and was the largest and most thoroughly equipped sugar plantation in the State of Florida. The owners worked 200 hands, and had 1,400 acres of sugar-cane in one field. Their sugar-mill and refinery contained all the modern appliances, and, at the commencement of the war, was worth half a million dollars. Soon after the breaking out of hostilities, most of the slaves were sent to Louisiana, and work on the plantation was abandoned. During the last year of the war, a Federal gunboat entered the

Manatee Bay, and a boat's crew, commanded by an officer, blew up the sugar-house and set fire to the refinery. The destruction was complete ; and to-day may be seen the ponderous fly-wheel of the engine, broken shafts and crumbling walls—sad mementos of the event. The family mansion, a large two-story brick structure, with galleries around three sides of both stories, escaped the hand of the destroyer. Although bearing the finger-marks of time, it is at this day, a substantial structure, and, with slight repairs, would weather the storms of another century. Connected with this old mansion is a history, now for the first time published.

Within these walls during the last days of the Southern Confederacy, when that fabric (on paper) was fast crumbling to pieces, Judah P. Benjamin, a fugitive from justice, and flying for his life under the assumed name of Charles Howard, was the guest for nearly two months of Captain Archibald McNeill, its then occupant. When on that memorable Sunday, in the spring of 1865, Jeff. Davis and his cabinet hastily fled from Richmond, Benjamin and Breckinridge struck out for the wilds of Florida, which seemed to offer a secure retreat. Arrived at Gainsville, Breckinridge sought refuge on the Atlantic coast, and Benjamin, under the guidance of Captain L. G. Leslie, started for the Gulf coast, *via* Tampa, and arrived safely at the mansion of Captain McNeill. After remaining nearly two months at Captain McNeill's, Benjamin was conveyed in a boat to Manatee, and from thence to Sarasoto Bay in a horse-cart, by Rev. E. Glazier, of Manatee; from thence to Cape Florida in a small sail-boat, commanded by Captain Fred. Tresca, also a resident of Manatee. At Cape Florida a larger boat was procured, and after several hair-breadth escapes from Federal gunboats and the perils of the sea, Captain Tresca landed his charge safely on one of the islands of the Bahama group, and returned to Manatee $1,500 richer than when he left home. Benjamin reached England safely, where he has acquired fame and fortune. Should this page by chance meet his eye, he will no doubt be pleased to learn that Captain McNeill, past threescore and ten, has retired from active life and settled in Manatee, surrounded by a large family. Captain Tresca, or Captain "Fred.," as he is called by his friends, lives with his wife and two children on a small plantation near Braidentown. Although he counts his years away up among the nineties, he is still a well-preserved "old salt." Rev. E. Glazier is still a resident of Manatee, and looks as though he had renewed his lease of life for another half century. Judas betrayed his Master for the paltry sum of thirty pieces of silver. Twenty-five thousand dollars was the price offered by the United States Government for the *corpus* of the fugitive.

The example of Judas was not followed by those who assisted Benjamin to escape.

There are more than a thousand acres of the rich hammock land belonging to this plantation for sale at from $15 to $25 per acre, according to location. , When the fact that it cost originally $75 per acre to clear this land, is taken into consideration, it will be seen that the price at which it is now offered is very low, and places it within the reach of persons of small means. The land will be sold in lots to suit purchasers.

Adjoining the grounds of the Patten mansion is the residence of Hamet J. Craig, who has a young orange grove of three hundred trees and ten acres of hammock land under cultivation. Five miles further on, in a north-easterly direction, is Oak Hill, the former residence of Major W. I. Turner. At this place the major has a bearing orange grove of several hundred trees, and also one of the most promising six-years-old groves of six hundred trees to be found in the Manatee region. Adjoining Major Turner is the grove of Walter Tresca, just coming into bearing, and near by is the young grove of Mr. William Gillett.

Terraceia Island, separated from Snead's Island by a narrow channel, is bounded on the west by Tampa Bay, on the north by Frog Creek, and on the east by Terraceia Bay. This island contains several tracts of excellent hammock land, most of which is under improvement. On this island are located the bearing orange groves of Messrs. Hallock, Lennard and Williams; Messrs. Kennedy, Howard, Gifford, Watkins, Hobart, Patten and Wyatt are also located on this island. Judge Cessna, of Gainesville, has recently purchased a plantation on the island, and will soon locate there. Other persons on the line of the Transit Railroad having become disgusted with frost and ice, are seeking homes in the Manatee region. On the mainland, on the east side, and about midway of Terraceia Bay, is the plantation of Mr. John Craig. Mr. Craig raises the finest cane and has the reputation of making the best sugar in Manatee County.

A short distance north of Terraceia Island, on the mainland, Hernando De Soto, fresh from the conquest of Peru, where he was associated with Francisco Pizarro, landed his troops in the latter part of May, 1539. He sailed from Havana on Sunday, May 18th, 1539, with his troops embarked in five large ships, two caravels and two brigantines. The disastrous fate of his predecessors in Florida cast no gloom on the mind of De Soto, and his assurances of success imparted confidence to those who accompanied him. He had never been defeated in battle, and was believed by his soldiers to be invincible. His officers were men of valor and ripe experience, and his troops were well disciplined, a majority of them having served in many campaigns, and all were well acquainted with Indian warfare.

His wife, Dona Isabella, did not share his enthusiasm, and desired to accompany him and share the dangers she believed he was about to encounter; but De Soto strenuously opposed her wishes, and encouraged her to believe that the time of reunion was not far distant. The conquest of Florida appeared to De Soto to be an easy task, from which he could soon return with large accessions of wealth and glory.

Contrary and baffling winds kept the squadron tossing about in the Gulf of Mexico for several days. De Soto and his troops obtained their first view of the Land of Flowers on the morning of the 25th day of May, and in the afternoon of the same day they came to anchor about two leagues from the shore. The shoals which extended along the coast prevented the ships from coming nearer. They had, in the meantime, been discovered by the natives, who had kindled beacon-fires along the beach, now known as Pinellas, as signals to collect their forces and be in readiness to repel their enemies. De Soto's vessels were anchored off the mouth of Tampa Bay, called by the Spaniards the Bay of Espiritu Santo.

The Natchez, who inhabited the neighboring country, were governed by a chief named Ucita,

whose hatred of the Spaniards is easily explained.
When Pamphilo de Narvaez visited this region in
1528, he was kindly received and hospitably en-
tertained by the Chief Ucita, and a treaty of
peace between them was formed ; yet, on a very
slight pretense, the wily and bloodthirsty Pamphilo caused the chief's nose to be cut off, and
his aged mother to be torn to pieces by dogs!
Hence, the reason why Ucita displayed implaca-
ble resentment in his behavior to De Soto and his
companions in arms.

Thus, it will be seen that from the earliest history of our country, the aborigines have been
treated with the most impolitic and unchristian-
like barbarity; and it is highly probable that
much of that ferocity which characterizes the Indians of the far West at this time, may be ascribed
to the harsh and merciless treatment which their
ancestors received from the early Spanish ex-
plorers, who acted on the principle that the Indians had no rights that a white man was bound to
respect.

Wishing to avoid a collision with the Indians
at that time, De Soto weighed anchor, and pro-
ceeded with his fleet two leagues further up the
bay, where he disembarked his troops in boats. The
place where he landed was on the eastern shore
of Hillsborough Bay, above the mouth of the
Little Manatee River, and near the line which
separates Hillsborough and Manatee Counties.

The Indians being anxious to get rid of De Soto and his followers, informed them that *El Dorado*, for which they were seeking, was further northward. De Soto sent his ships back to Havana, and commenced his toilsome march overland, which ended with his death and burial in the Mississippi River, on the 5th day of June, 1542, three years and one month after the date of his arrival in Tampa Bay.

CHAPTER IV.

"Sunnyside"—Orange and Banana Groves—Lemons and Limes—Coffee Trees and Pine-apples—California Grapes—Quality of the Land—Mode of Cultivation—Florida, Past, Present and Future—Increased Production—Better and Cheaper Transportation—Interrogatories and Answers.

Having given the reader a hasty outline of the Manatee region, I will add a brief *resume* of my personal experience at "Sunnyside" during the past eighteen months. On my arrival in Braidentown, in the fall of 1879, my land was a "howling wilderness." At this time I have a young orange grove of six hundred trees, sixty lemon, fifteen lime, ten guava, half a dozen olive, two soft-shell almond, twenty coffee, four each Japan plum and persimmon, two pomegranate, two cocoa-nut and four Le Conte pear trees, all of which are growing luxuriantly. I also have one acre in bananas and sixty pine-apple plants, both of which will bear fruit next year. Around the fence inclosing my house lot, I have sixty California grape-vines of the choicest varieties, viz.: Flaming Tokay, White Muscat of Alexandria, Mission and Rose of Peru. The vines are looking well, and will bear fruit next year.

46

From a Photograph by F. PINARD, Manatee and Tampa.

SUNNYSIDE COTTAGE,

The Residence of SAMUEL C. UPHAM, Braidentown, Florida.

The land on which I am located is spruce-pine, interspersed with water-oak and scrub palmetto, which would be pronounced by the average Floridian worthless. I had at the commencement, and still have, abiding faith in the white sand of Florida with a mulatto sub-soil. No matter how white the surface, if underlied by a mulatto or yellow sub-soil, the citrus family will thrive. The foliage of my young trees is dark green, and their vigorous growth astonishes the "crackers," who predicted a failure. Owing to the mildness of the climate—my location being exempt from frost —my trees grew all last winter. My orange trees are set in parallel rows, thirty feet apart each way; the lemon and lime trees twenty-five feet apart; the bananas twelve feet, and the pine-apples two feet apart. I hoe my grove every two months, and plow it four times a year. Thus, by keeping the soil constantly tickled with the hoe, my trees laugh with a bountiful foliage. What I have done, can be performed by others. There is no secret about the matter. We welcome immigrants from the frigid North, from the prairies of the West, and from the lands beyond the sea. To all we say, come and tarry with us.

Florida, the first State belonging to the Union, discovered and settled by Europeans, has, during the past 350 years, been hustled about from pillar to post like a shuttle-cock. The repeated Indian wars from 1816 to 1858, rendered life so insecure, that the early settlers literally carried their lives in their hands. Is it then a matter of surprise that Florida is so sparsely populated? Mr. J. S. Adams, former Commissioner of Immigration, truthfully remarks: "The wonder truly is, not that she has not attained a more flourishing condition, but that she exists at all, and that her boundless forests, her lovely rivers and her beautiful lakes are not fast locked in the silent embrace of a moveless desolation." Since slavery, which rested like an incubus of original sin on the soil of Florida, has been removed, immigration has been pouring in from the North and the West, and from the isles of the ocean. Germany, Italy, France and England have each furnished their quota, and the forests along the line of the railroads, as well as those accessible by steamboats, are beginning to show the effects of an advanced civilization. The gigantic undertaking of draining Lake Okeechobee and the Everglades, together with the construction of a ship canal, connecting the Atlantic Ocean with the Gulf of Mexico, by Mr. Hamilton Disston, of Philadelphia, and his coadjutors, is proof positive that a new era is beginning to dawn on the Land of Flowers, and, ere many years, the southern portion of the State will be one vast orange grove, interspersed with the guava, lemon, lime, pine-apple and banana. I hear the skeptic say: "You will over-stock the market, and your fruit will not pay the cost of transportation." The orange *par excellence* can be grown *only* in the soil of Florida, therefore competition with foreign countries need not be feared. Florida will soon be able to supply the cities of the Mediterranean with a superior fruit to that grown on their own shores, and more cheaply. Increased production and transportation will cause a corresponding reduction in freight, and also insure greater and better facilities in the modes of transportation. There will also be a large reduction in price to the consumer, which will enable the man of limited means—in other words, the poor man—to indulge with the millionaire in the daily luxury of the golden apple of the Hesperides—the Florida orange. The above may be deemed by some persons chimerical, but time, the great arbiter of events, will solve the problem.

By every mail I am in receipt of letters asking all manner of questions in relation to the climate, soil, productions, etc., of this part of Florida. At first I cheerfully complied with the requests of my numerous correspondents, but the novelty has worn off, and the task has become slightly monotonous. Recently, I received a four-page cap-sheet letter from a gentleman in Utah Territory, to which was appended seventeen interrogatories in relation to the Gulf Coast of South Florida. That straw broke the camel's back, and, in reply to the following question: "I see by the last census that Manatee County has a population of over 4,000, and not a death recorded for 1880. Do people ever die there?" I wrote immediately, "Hardly ever. When we want to start a grave-yard, we kill a man." I am firmly impressed with the belief that my Mormon correspondent, with a "family of ten persons," will not immigrate to the Land of Flowers. Below will be found twenty-five questions in relation to Florida, from correspondents the "wide world over," with answers appended :

1st. "At any time of the year do you have severe storms of thunder and lightning?"

During the rainy season, thunder showers, accompanied by lightning, frequently occur, but they are not more severe than in the Northern and Western States.

2d. "Are venomous reptiles numerous?"

During my residence and travels in Florida, I have never seen a rattlesnake; I have seen a few moccasin, garter, coachwhip and blacksnakes. The two latter are harmless, and are seldom killed by the natives. Alligators are not numerous in this vicinity, and are comparatively harmless. Scorpions and centipedes are seldom met with. Their sting is no more severe than that of a bee.

3d. " Is the land about Braidentown sandy or clayey ?"

The land on the margin of the bay is sandy; further back in the hammock, the soil is dark gray and chocolate color, underlied with clay and limestone.

4th. "Are the people mostly Northern ?"

Like an Englishman's favorite beverage, they are 'alf-and-'alf.

5th. "What is the name of your nearest town of any importance ?"

Have no towns of "importance" in this section of the country; they are in the womb of time—not hatched yet.

6th. "What is the character of your society?"

Mixed.

7th. " Do you consider Florida as healthy as California ?"

I consider this Manatee region the sanitarium of the world. A more healthful spot cannot be found on God's footstool.

8th. " Do malarial fevers prevail in your section any time during the year ?"

In the rich, low hammock lands, where vegetation is rank, malarial fevers exist in the fall of the year. Chills and fever here yield more readily to proper medical treatment than in the West. Pine land is exempt from malaria.

9th. " Does the summer heat prove enervating ?"

That depends on a man's constitution.   If born tired, yes.

10th. "Is it true that the summer weather with you is more pleasant—less oppressive—than at the North?"

Yes; the thermometer rarely registers more than 96°.   It reached that point only twice last summer.

11th. "Are the nights in summer always cool?"

Generally; sometimes cooler than in the winter.

12th. "Can you work out of doors during the day in summer time?"

Yes, when it does not rain.   I have not seen a day too hot to work out of doors since my arrival in Florida.

13th. "Do the crops of vegetables and grass burn under the summer sun?"

We don't raise vegetables in the summer.   Our vegetables are grown in the winter and spring, when the land at the North is locked fast in the embrace of frost and ice.   The grass here is very nutritious, and large herds of cattle fatten on it. This section of country supplies Cuba with beef.

14th. "Are insects—fleas and mosquitoes— more troublesome than at the North?"

Fleas sometimes make it lively with us; but there are fewer mosquitoes in this locality than in a majority of the Northern States.

15th. "Do you consider Manatee County one of the best to settle in?"

It suits me better than any other part of Florida. You might go further and fare worse.

16th. "Do you think the Gulf Coast equal to the Atlantic Coast for climate, health, etc.?"

Yes; far superior.

17th. "What is the price of land in your section?"

That depends upon quality and location. Here, in the settlement of Braidentown, land is selling at from $25 to $100 per acre. A short distance back of the town, pine land can be purchased at from $1.50 to $5 per acre; and hammock land at $10 per acre. Across the bay, nearly opposite Manatee, on the Patten plantation, good hammock land, once under cultivation, can be purchased at from $15 to $25 per acre, according to location. This land is being rapidly metamorphosed into vegetable gardens, whose products—tomatoes, cucumbers, beans, peas, etc.—reach the Northern markets during the month of March.

18th. "What are the business prospects for a new-comer?"

That will depend a great deal on the "new-comer." Come, investigate and judge for yourself.

19. "Can sugar-cane be grown to advantage in your neighborhood? and what amount of sugar can be made to the acre?"

The Manatee region is the natural home of the

sugar-cane. Here it tassels, and consequently fully matures. Florida is the only State of the Union in which the cane tassels. When the Cofield and Davis, now Patten plantation, was in full operation, the average product was two hogsheads of sugar to the acre. The cane here ratoons from six to eight years.

20th. "What is the cost of clearing land?"

That depends on the quality of the land. The average pine land can be cleared and grubbed at from $10 to $20 per acre. Hammock land will cost double that price.

21st. "Can lumber be had on the Manatee, and if so, at what price?"

Heart-pine lumber, suitable for fencing or building purposes, can be had here at $15 per M. Light wood posts can be purchased at $10 per hundred.

22d. "What is the price of labor in your vicinity?"

Colored laborers can be hired at from $15 to $20 per month, with board or rations. The price is $1 per day when the laborer boards himself.

23d. "Are fish, oysters and game plentiful?"

Our rivers and bayous are literally alive with mullet—the mackerel of the South. Sea-trout (black bass), jack-fish, sheepshead, red-fish, angel-fish, drum and pompino can also be had in abundance in the water around Palm Key, at the mouth of the bay. Oysters and clams of a superior quality can be had in Terraceia and Sarasoto Bays. Deer, squirrels, quail and wild turkeys abound in the adjoining hammocks.

24th. "Can you refer me to any person in your vicinity whose health has been benefited by the climate?"

Yes; several. Rev. Edmund Lee, of Manatee, arrived here forty-five years ago, a confirmed invalid; in fact, nearly gone with pulmonary consumption. On his first arrival he was so weak that it required considerable effort to pull a mullet off a grid-iron. The healthfulness of the climate, together with out-door exercise and a clear conscience, have enabled him to fight the flesh and the devil successfully to the present time. He is at this time a well-preserved patriarch of seventy-two years; has outlived two wives, and bids fair to remain many years longer on this side of Jordan.

Mr. John M. Helm, residing some three miles south-east of Braidentown, arrived from Windsor, Ind., about four years since. He also was nearly gone with consumption. One lung was hepatized, and on the other a tubercle formed, and discharged after his arrival here. Physicians at the West pronounced his case hopeless—beyond the reach of medicine—and recommended the climate of Florida as a last resort. He is now a well man, and can hoe more orange trees in a day, and hoe them better, than any man I know in Florida.

Two years ago I arrived here, clad in porous-plasters, suffering with chronic rheumatism. Two months later I was as frisky as a lamb in spring time. I am convinced that my old complaint has left me never to return, so long as I remain here. I could record other cases, but the above must suffice for the present.

25th. " State the most direct route to Braiden-town."

By rail to Cedar Key, the terminus of railroad communication, thence by the boats of the Tampa Steamship Company to this place. A boat leaves Cedar Key on Monday and Friday afternoon of each week, and arrives at Braidentown early on the following morning. Fare, $8. The above is the advertised programme, but it is sometimes changed to suit wind and weather. Captains Jackson and Doane are thorough seamen, and do everything in their power to render passengers comfortable. Whatever may be the opinion of travelers in regard to the speed and ` accommodations of the boats, they will unanimously agree that the fare—$8 for a distance of less than 100 miles—is *first-class.* A line of light draught, modern-built and comfortably fitted-up steam-boats, between Cedar Key and Braidentown, would be liberally patronized. Shall we have the boats? Echo repeats the question.

CHAPTER V.

FLORIDA LETTER PUBLISHED IN A CALIFORNIA PAPER—
EDITORIAL REMARKS—THE "FOUNTAIN OF YOUTH"—
THE MANATEE RIVER AND ITS SURROUNDINGS—TROPI-
CAL FRUITS—GAME AND FISH—THE SPORTSMAN'S PAR-
ADISE—LETTER TO THE EDITRESS OF THE "PHILADEL-
PHIA SUNDAY TIMES"—THE LAND OF PROMISE—
SUNSTROKE AND HYDROPHOBIA UNKNOWN—COOL
NIGHTS DURING THE "DOG DAYS"—PREPARING THE
LAND AND PLANTING AN ORANGE GROVE—THE FLO-
RIDA ORANGE—ROUTE TO THE MANATEE—CLIMATE OF
THE GULF COAST OF SOUTH FLORIDA—RECORD OF
THERMOMETER AND RAINFALL FOR THE YEAR 1880—
NO FROST—REPORT IN RELATION TO THE EFFECTS OF
THE FREEZE ON THE ATLANTIC COAST IN DECEMBER
LAST.

As THE following letters and communications
have a direct bearing on the Manatee region, the
reader will pardon their republication. Among
the chaff perchance may be found a few grains of
information that will pay for the perusal. The
first letter was written to a personal friend in the
city of New York, who forwarded it to the San
Francisco *Examiner*. It was first published in that
paper with the following editorial remarks:

"Old Californians are not unfamiliar with the name of Mr.
Samuel C. Upham, an editor upon this coast in the early

days, and, of late, the author of a work entitled *Voyage to California via Cape Horn, and Scenes in El Dorado in* 1849 *and* 1850. We are permitted to copy a letter from that gentleman, written in his humorous style, and addressed to an old Californian friend, which may prove of interest to others."

PHILADELPHIA, *June 16th, 1879.*

FRIEND C——: I owe you a letter, and the following is what I have to say: You are aware that I went South last winter for the benefit of my health, and that I returned in the spring as frisky as a lamb. The late hot weather has pulled me down considerably, and I sigh for the Land of Flowers, where Ponce de Leon searched for the fountain of youth, and Upham found it. I was so charmed with the climate of the Gulf Coast of South Florida, that, while there last winter, I purchased 225 acres of land on the Manatee River, fifty miles south of Tampa, and Mrs. U. and myself are going down to that land of promise the coming fall, to plant an orange grove, and sit under our own vine, orange and eucalyptus trees. It is a delightful country, away down below "frost line," where the pine-apple, banana, guava, sapadillo, pomegranate, date, cocoa-nut, orange, lime and lemon grow almost spontaneously. The rivers are overflowing with fish, and the forests are overrun with game. Roasted wild turkeys run about with carving-knives and forks sticking in their backs, and ask to be eaten. The country now is a trifle wild, but will soon become tamed and civilized. The people are hospitable, and welcome all classes ôf strangers, with the exception of "carpet-baggers." They have been tried and found wanting.

I shall locate in the village—if two stores and four houses can be dignified by that name—of Braidentown, Manatee County, Florida. The place is scarcely twelve months old, but is bound to be heard from—after I locate there. The

climate is delightful—sort of an earthly Paradise. The thermometer during the winter months ranges from 70° to 75°,
and in summer rarely exceeds 90°, with a sea-breeze blowing
constantly either from the Atlantic or the Gulf. The nights
in summer are invariably cool, and one can lie comfortably
under blankets during " dog days.'

I do not expect to make money in Florida, but I do
pect to enjoy better health than in this city; hence the reason
of my exodus. I shall, first off, plant an orange grove of 500
trees, which, in eight years, barring accidents, ought to yield me
a handsome revenue. Should I "shuffle off this mortal coil "
before these orange trees commence bearing, I shall feel dis-
appointed—that's all. I think the change will give me a
renewed lease of life; and, as I intend to plant three-years-old
trees, I think the chances are rather in my favor. The Good
Book says : " What does it profit a man if he gain the whole
world and lose his own life ?" I am not prepared to "hand
in my checks " just yet; hence my change of base. I have
been watching and praying the past four or five years for the
"good time coming " to put in an appearance, but it has not
arrived, and will not, I fear, during my sojourn in this vale
of tears. I have a mortal dread of the poor-house. In Florida
that institution is unknown. My eldest son will take charge
of my store and laboratory in this city, so the business will
go on without interruption. As I have spun out this letter to
a great length, I will say domino.

Truly yours,

S. C. UPHAM.

The following letter was published originally
in Taggart's *Philadelphia Sunday Times,* under
the following caption : " Life in Florida. Inter-
esting letter from Samuel C. Upham, formerly of

Philadelphia, but now located in Florida, addressed to our lady editress. Hints to those who may wish to visit the Flowery Land."

SUNNYSIDE COTTAGE,

BRAIDENTOWN, FLA., *June 8th, 1880.*

MY DEAR MRS. BLADEN: In the *Sunday Times* of the 30th ult., you say:

" Mr. Samuel C. Upham, whose popular songs and wonderful California experiences render him a Philadelphia celebrity, has a large plantation near Jacksonville."

It is pleasing to know, when one is far away, that he is not entirely forgotten by his friends; but you are slightly mistaken when you say I own a large orange plantation near Jacksonville. I am located on the Manatee River, some eight miles above its entrance into Tampa Bay, on the Gulf coast of South Florida, in latitude 27½°, and below " frost line." I visited Jacksonville and all the towns and landings on the St. Johns, Halifax and Matanzas Rivers, and also " did" the Suwanee pretty thoroughly before locating in Braidentown. I prefer this part of Florida to the Atlantic coast for the following reasons: Heathfulness of climate, purity of water and immunity from frost and insects. My health has improved wonderfully since my arrival in the Land of Flowers, and I am pretty thoroughly convinced that I have obtained a new lease of life. The sea breezes that fan my brow at morning, noon and night, act as a tonic on my enfeebled constitution, and I am daily gaining strength and muscle. I have to-day worked six hours in my banana grove, with the thermometer at 90° in the shade, without experiencing any inconvenience from the heat. The heat is so modified by the constant sea breeze that one can work in the sun at all hours of the day and at all seasons of the year. Sunstroke and hydrophobia are unknown here. This statement can be taken *without* salt. In midsummer the nights are invariably cool. Blankets at night are the rule, not the exception. This much about location and climate; now, a few words about *that* orange grove.

My *ranch* is new, and consequently rather crude. When I located here in November last, a large portion of it was a "howling wilderness." Since that time, I have felled the trees, piled the logs, burned the brush, grubbed and fenced fifteen acres, on ten acres of which I am now setting out 500 two-years-old sweet seedling orange trees, which I hope to live long enough to see bear fruit. Some two months since, I set out 200 banana plants, and they are doing remarkably well; many of the stalks are six feet in height. They will bear fruit in about eighteen months. I also have a patch of sixty pine-apple plants which will bear fruit next year. I have a few coffee and tea plants, Japan plum and persimmon, pomegranate, almond and olive trees that are growing luxuriantly. I brought with me from Philadelphia, half a dozen cocoanuts, which I planted on the 1st of November last, and had given up all hope of ever seeing them sprout, when, to my great surprise, some two weeks since, two of them threw up sprouts. They are now one foot high, and are growing vigorously. The guava thrives admirably here. I have several trees, and expect soon to luxuriate on guava jelly of my own manufacture. I will send you a few sample boxes.

Have you ever eaten a Florida orange, fresh plucked, that ripened on the tree? If not, visit Florida, and enjoy the greatest luxury of your life. It is the fruit *par excellence*— fit food for the gods. I have, in the course of my somewhat eventful life, eaten oranges in the groves of the Mediterranean, South America, Mexico and the West Indies, but none can compare with the orange grown in this State. Our soil is peculiarly adapted to the growth and maturity of the *per-*

feet orange.   No other soil can produce it.   The West India
and Louisiana seedling orange tree is wonderfully improved
by being transplanted in Florida soil.   South Florida will,
ere long, be one vast orange grove, and will supply the world
with her incomparable fruit.   She will supply the Mediterranean ports with better oranges than can possibly be raised in
that country.   Won't that be "carrying coals to Newcastle?"
I may not live to see the above prediction verified, but there
are persons living at 'this time who will.

If any of your numerous friends think it would be a good
thing to have an orange grove, advise them to visit the Gulf
coast of South Florida before locating elsewhere.   Also tell
them to drop in at Braidentown.   They may go further and
fare worse.   The most direct route to this place is by rail to
Cedar Key, the present terminus of railroad communication,
thence by steamer down the coast.   The mail steamers leave
Cedar Key twice a week for this place and Tampa.   Leave
Cedar Key at 4 o'clock P. M. on Monday and Friday of each
week, and arrive at Braidentown at 7 o'clock the following
morning.   *Au revoir.*   S. C. UPHAM.

The following communication was published in
the *Florida Agriculturist* in January last, under
the caption of the " *Climate of the Gulf Coast of
South Florida.*"

Having kept a record of the state of the thermometer at
6 o'clock A. M., 12 o'clock M. and 6 o'clock P. M. at Braidentown, Manatee County, Florida, from the 1st day of January to the 31st day of December, 1880, inclusive, 1 herewith
inclose you a synopsis of the same for publication in the
Agriculturist, with the hope that it may interest your numerous readers, especially those in the Northern and Western
States who are seeking homes in

The land of the orange and guava,
The pine-apple, date and cassava.

I also send a statement of the rainfall for the year 1880.

TEMPERATURE.

Average temperature at 6 o'clock A. M., . . .	. 71⅓°
Average temperature at 12 o'clock M., . . .	83⅔°
Average temperature at 6 o'clock P. M., . .	. 78⅞°
Highest temperature at 12 o'clock M., July 1st and August 26th, ...	96°
Lowest temperature at 6 o'clock A. M., Dec. 31st,	. 38°

RAINFALL.

	Rainy Days.	Clear Days.	Cloudy and Partly Cloudy Days.
January, ...	5	19	12
February, ...	3	24	5
March, ...	3	24	7
April, ...	1	29	1
May, ...	12	4	27
June, ...	18	8	22
July, ...	12	6	25
August, ...	18	8	23
September, ...	13	15	15
October, ...	10	19	12
November, ...	3	15	15
December, ...	6	17	14
Total, ...	104	188	177

Rainfall during year, ... 69½ inches.

At least one-half the days classed as "cloudy and partly cloudy" were clear one-half of the day, and a majority of the "rainy days" were clear three-fourths of the day. Dur-

ing the gale on the 29th and 30th of last August, which was
so destructive on the Atlantic coast of the State, rain fell
here almost uninterruptedly for nearly forty-eight hours, but
the wind did little or no damage. The rainfall during the
two days was six and one-half inches, the heaviest of the
season. I have resided here during the past fourteen months,
and, up to this time (January 7th, 1881), there has been *no
frost*, and my tropical fruits and plants have grown luxuriantly every month of the year. The year just closed, in its
dying throes, kicked the mercury in the thermometer down
to 38°, and a slight frost occurred on the opposite side of the
Manatee River, and also in the hammock four or five miles
south-east of Braidentown. The water protection—being
surrounded on three sides by the aqueous fluid—has rendered
Braidentown *exempt from frost*.

Although the rainfall of 1880 has been some nine inches
in excess of the average rainfall in this State, I have passed
one of the most agreeable summers of my life. While the
denizens of the St. Johns and Atlantic coast are shivering in
the chilling blasts of winter, we on the Gulf coast of South
Florida are basking in the sun, with a temperature of 65° at
6 o'clock A. M., 75° at 12 o'clock M. and 70° at 6 o'clock
P. M. If any locality north of latitude 27½° can present a
more favorable record, Braidentown will yield the palm.
Nous verrons.

S. C. UPHAM.

SUNNYSIDE COTTAGE,
BRAIDENTOWN, FLA., Jan. 7th, 1881.

The following report, now for the first time
printed, explains itself:

SUNNYSIDE COTTAGE,
BRAIDENTOWN, FLA., *Feb. 5th, 1881.*

D. II. ELLIOTT, ESQ.,
See. "*Florida Fruit Growers' Association,*"
JACKSONVILLE, FLA.,

DEAR SIR: In the Report of the Proceedings of the Eighth Annual Meeting of the "Florida Fruit Growers' Association," held in Jacksonville on the 27 ult., and published in the *Daily Union* of that city on the following morning, the annexed resolution was published, with the name of your humble servant appended as one of the committee :

"*Resolved*, That a committee be appointed to investigate the effects of the late freeze on the orange and other fruits and vegetables; said committee to report to the secretary at Jacksonville at the earliest practicable moment."

Having received no official notice of my appointment to serve on the aforesaid committee, I have resolved myself into a committee of one, and have the honor to respectfully report as follows :

The old and trite aphorism—" If the mountain will not come to Mahomet, Mahomet must go to the mountain "—seems peculiarly applicable to the above resolution. Ergo, if the orange and other fruits of the citrus family will not thrive 'mid frost and ice, cultivate them in a more genial climate. With the experience of last fall and the present winter before me, together with a careful investigation of the climatology of Florida during the past fifty years, I have come to the conclusion that the fruits comprising the citrus family cannot be *successfully* cultivated in this State north of the 28th parallel of latitude, and the sooner and more widely this fact is promulgated, the better it will be for all persons interested or about to become interested in this laudable and growing industry. The fact that the late freeze killed the scale insects on the orange trees in middle and north Florida, is *cold* comfort for those engaged in orange culture. There are fruits better adapted to the climate of Florida north of latitude 28° than the orange, lemon, lime, guava, banana and pine-apple. Why, then, persist in endeavoring to cultivate those fruits with so dim a prospect of success? It is kicking against the pricks, hoping against hope. In conclusion, plant your orange, lemon, lime and banana groves below the 28th parallel of latitude, tickle the soil constantly with the hoe, and success will crown your efforts. So mote it be.

S. C. UPHAM.

METEOROLOGICAL.

*Record of the Thermometer and Rainfall at Braidentown,
Florida, for the month of January, 1880, with Remarks
in relation to Wind and Weather.*

Date.	6 o'clock A.M.	12 o'clock M.	6 o'clock P.M.	Wind at M.	Rainfall.	Remarks.
1	65	80	76	E.	⅛ in.	Cloudy A. M., clear P. M.
2	64	78	76	E.	......	Clear.
3	68	82	74	E.	......	A. M. clear, P. M. cloudy.
4	64	80	77	E.	......	Clear with strong E. wind.
5	66	80	74	S. E.	......	Clear A. M., cloudy P. M.
6	64	80	74	E.	......	Clear.
7	62	80	72	N. W.	......	"
8	62	78	70	W.	......	Cloudy.
9	62	82	72	W.	......	Clear.
10	61	84	75	E.	......	"
11	62	82	72	E.	......	"
12	62	82	74	E.	......	"
13	64	74	70	N. E.	......	"
14	58	78	73	E.	......	"
15	58	78	72	S.	......	"
16	55	86	68	E.	......	"
17	58	78	72	W.	......	"
18	55	76	66	N. W.	......	"
19	52	74	70	E.	......	"
20	53	78	68	S. W.	......	"
21	56	78	70	S.	......	Cloudy.
22	64	76	72	S.	2 in.	Rain A. M., clear P. M.
23	65	82	56	W.	⅛ in.	" " " "
24	54	58	58	N. W.	¾ in.	Clear A. M., rain P. M.
25	58	73	70	E.	......	Cloudy.
26	71	78	70	S. W.	½ in.	Rain A. M., clear P. M.
27	64	68	62	W.	......	Cloudy.
28	58	66	63	N. W.	......	"
29	58	80	72	E.	......	Clear.
30	63	86	70	S. E.	......	"
31	62	80	70	W.	......	"
Sums,	1,788	2,315	2,168	......	3½ in.	
Av'ge	57⅓	74¾	70	......	......	

Lowest temperature at 6 o'clock A. M., 19th inst...............................52°
Highest   "   12   "   M., 16th and 30th insts.................86°

METEOROLOGICAL.

Record of the Thermometer and Rainfall at Braidentown, Florida, for the month of February, 1880, with Remarks in relation to Wind and Weather.

Date.	6 o'clock A. M.	12 o'clock M.	6 o'clock P. M.	Wind at M.	Rainfall.	Remarks.
1	64	76	68	N. W.	......	Cloudy. [all day.
2	62	80	73	S.	⅛ in.	Rain at night. Strong wind
3	66	70	62	N. W.	......	Wind has blown a gale all day
4	46	72	58	S. E.	......	Clear A. M., cloudy P. M.
5	56	80	74	E.	⅛ in.	Rain during night, clear all
6	52	68	62	E.	......	Cloudy. [day.
7	55	74	64	E.	......	Clear.
8	62	80	70	W.	......	"
9	60	74	68	E.	......	"
10	58	86	72	W.	......	"
11	57	83	76	E.	......	"
12	62	82	74	W.	......	"
13	66	79	74	S.	......	Clear. Wind blowing a gale.
14	72	80	75	S.	1 in.	Rain during night, cloudy all
15	63	74	63	N. E.	......	Clear. [day.
16	49	78	68	E.	......	"
17	58	82	76	E.	......	"
18	64	86	74	S. W.	......	"
19	63	84	70	N. W.	......	"
20	63	85	72	E.	......	"
21	62	77	70	W.	......	"
22	67	76	66	W.	......	"
23	53	79	69	W.	......	"
24	56	81	70	E.	......	"
25	60	80	72	S. E.	......	"
26	62	80	74	S.	......	"
27	58	88	74	N. E.	......	"
28	60	82	72	W.	......	"
29	68	87	74	S. E.	......	"
Sums,	1,744	2,303	2,034	......	1¼ in.	
Av'ge	60⅛	79½	70⅛	......	......	

Lowest temperature at 6 o'clock A. M., 4th inst..............................46°
Highest   "   12   "   M., 27th inst...............................83°

METEOROLOGICAL.

Record of the Thermometer and Rainfall at Braidentown, Florida, for the month of March, 1880, with Remarks in relation to Wind and Weather.

Date.	6 o'clock A. M.	12 o'clock M.	6 o'clock P. M.	Wind at M.	Rainfall.	Remarks.
1	60	79	74	S.	......	Clear.
2	64	82	79	N. W.	......	"
3	68	80	76	S. W.	......	"
4	67	82	73	S. W.	......	"
5	64	83	75	S. W.	......	"
6	64	83	76	W.	......	"
7	73	83	76	S. W.	......	"
8	68	81	76	S. W.	......	"
9	76	82	78	S. W.	......	"
10	74	84	73	S. W.	......	"
11	68	84	73	S. W.	......	"
12	71	86	73	S. W.	......	"
13	67	86	73	S.	......	"
14	72	86	73	S. W.	......	"
15	69	85	73	S.	......	"
16	70	84	78	S.	......	Cloudy.
17	70	84	76	S. W.	......	"
18	73	84	73	S. W.	......	Clear.
19	76	84	78	S. W.	......	"
20	76	83	74	E.	⅛ in.	Rain during night, cloudy all [day.
21	67	80	74	E.	......	Cloudy.
22	65	81	72	E.	1⅛ in.	Rain during night, cloudy all [day.
23	64	75	74	E.	......	Cloudy.
24	63	80	75	N. W.	......	Clear.
25	63	83	78	E.	......	"
26	65	82	78	E.	......	"
27	68	82	77	S. W.	......	"
28	75	72	72	W.	1⅛ in.	Rain A. M., cloudy P. M.
29	69	73	69	W.	......	Clear.
30	62	76	74	S. E.	......	"
31	52	76	74	E.	......	"
Sums,	2,093	2,530	2,359	......	¼ in.	
Av'ge	67½	81¼	76⅛	......	......	

Lowest temperature at 6 o'clock A. M., 31st inst...............52°
Highest " 12 " M., 12th, 13th and 14th insts.......86°

METEOROLOGICAL.

Record of the Thermometer and Rainfall at Braidentown, Florida, for the month of April, 1880, with Remarks in relation to Wind and Weather.

Date.	6 o'clock A. M.	12 o'clock M.	6 o'clock P. M.	Wind at M.	Rainfall.	Remarks.
1	65	81	72	W.	......	Clear.
2	60	79	75	W.	......	"
3	67	82	76	S. W.	......	"
4	70	80	75	S. W.	......	"
5	69	81	76	S. W.	......	"
6	65	83	76	S. W.	......	"
7	63	82	79	S. W.	......	"
8	68	82	78	S. W.	......	"
9	70	77	69	S. W.	¼ in.	Cloudy, with rain in the
10	59	76	68	N. W.	......	Clear. [evening
11	65	79	75	S. W.	......	"
12	65	78	76	S. E.	......	"
13	58	77	75	S. W.	......	"
14	62	88	80	E.	......	"
15	65	83	78	N. W	......	"
16	68	83	78	N. W.	......	"
17	70	84	78	W.	......	"
18	75	85	79	S. W.	......	"
19	74	85	81	W.	......	"
20	76	86	85	W.	......	"
21	73	86	82	W.	......	"
22	69	86	81	S. W.	......	"
23	72	85	79	S. W.	......	"
24	73	87	80	S. W.	......	"
25	73	86	79	S. W.	......	"
26	72	87	84	S. W.	......	"
27	73	86	84	S. W.	......	"
28	76	88	85	S. W.	......	"
29	74	87	82	S. W.	......	"
30	76	88	86	S. W.	......	"
Sums,	2,065	2,497	2,351	......	¼ in.	
Av'ge	68⅚	83¼	78⅓	......	......	

Lowest temperature at 6 o'clock A. M., 13th inst........................580
Highest " 12 " M., 14th, 28th and 30th insts.........880

METEOROLOGICAL.

Record of the Thermometer and Rainfall at Braidentown, Florida, for the month of May, 1880, with Remarks in relation to Wind and Weather.

Date.	6 o'clock A. M.	12 o'clock M.	6 o'clock P. M.	Wind at M.	Rainfall.	Remarks
1	73	89	86	E.	......	Clear.
2	72	89	79	S. E.	½ in.	Cloudy, with rain P. M.
3	72	80	79	S. E.	......	" with Scotch mist.
4	78	84	84	S. W.	......	Clear.
5	75	79	81	S. E.	......	Cloudy, with Scotch mist.
6	74	83	83	E.	......	Cloudy.
7	74	90	74	E.	1 in.	Rain during P. M. and night.
8	75	80	76	E.	2¼ in.	" " " "
9	76	85	78	E.	......	Cloudy, with Scotch mist.
10	74	87	86	S. W.	......	Partly cloudy.
11	73	87	79	S. W.	1 in.	Rain in the afternoon.
12	75	78	78	S. W.	1½ in.	" " "
13	72	83	83	S. W.	......	Cloudy.
14	75	84	83	S. W.	......	"
15	75	83	81	E.	......	Cloudy; wind blowing a gale.
16	72	85	79	E.	......	" " "
17	70	86	80	E.	......	Cloudy.
18	73	87	83	E.	......	"
19	73	90	84	E.	......	"
20	75	90	82	S. E.	½ in.	Rain during P. M. and night.
21	75	90	80	S. E.	1 in.	" " " "
22	75	79	78	S. E.	2 in.	" " the day.
23	78	86	78	S. E.	1 in.	" " "
24	78	86	78	S. E.	¼ in.	" " "
25	76	75	78	S. E.	½ in.	" " "
26	76	88	78	S. E.	......	Cloudy, with Scotch mist.
27	75	89	86	S. E.	......	Partly cloudy.
28	76	89	89	S. E.	......	" "
29	76	90	87	S. E.	¼ in.	Rain during night, day clear
30	78	95	87	S. E.	......	Clear.
31	80	91	86	S. E.	......	"
Sums,	2,319	2,657	2,523	......	11¾ in	.
Av'ge	74¾	85¾	81⅓	......	......	

Lowest temperature at 6 o'clock A. M., 2d, 3d, 13th and 16th insts...72°
Highest   "   . 12   "   M , 30th inst............................95°

METEOROLOGICAL.

Record of the Thermometer and Rainfall at Braidentown, Florida, for the month of June, 1880, with Remarks in relation to Wind and Weather.

Date.	6 o'clock A. M.	12 o'clock M.	6 o'clock P. M.	Wind at M.	Rainfall.	Remarks.
1	80	88	84	S. E.	½ in.	Cloudy.
2	82	82	81	S. E.	½ in.	"
3	80	87	85	W.	½ in.	Rain in the afternoon.
4	78	91	85	S. E.	......	Cloudy, with Scotch mist.
5	80	89	82	S. E.	1½ in.	Rain in the afternoon.
6	81	87	80	S. E.	½ in.	" " "
7	79	90	85	S. W.	......	Clear.
8	80	89	87	S. W.	......	"
9	82	91	90	S. W.	1 in.	Rain in evening.
10	78	92	78	S. W.	1 in.	" " afternoon.
11	80	90	78	S. W.	¼ in.	" " "
12	79	92	88	S. W.	......	Clear.
13	82	90	88	S. W.	......	"
14	84	91	87	W.	......	"
15	86	92	88	W.	......	"
16	85	91	87	W.	......	"
17	79	89	88	S. W.	1 in.	Rain A. M., clear P. M.
18	80	88	88	S. W.	......	Clear.
19	77	79	83	S. W.	¼ in.	Rain A. M., clear P. M.
20	80	86	76	E.	......	Cloudy.
21	76	80	78	S. W.	⅛ in.	"
22	74	88	80	S. E.	¼ in.	Rain P. M. and at night.
23	78	87	84	S.	1 in,	Rain during night.
24	78	90	84	S. E.	......	Cloudy.
25	78	87	86	S.	1/18 in.	Rain during afternoon.
26	80	92	86	S. E.		Shower during afternoon.
27	86	91	84	S. W.		Light shower in afternoon.
28	82	88	89	S. W.	¼ in.	" " " "
29	81	86	86	S. W.		" " " "
30	83	94	86	S. W.		" " " "
Sums,	2,408	2,657	2,531	......	8⅞ in.	
Av'ge	80¼	88½	84⅓	......	......	

Lowest temperature at 6 o'clock A. M., 22d inst..............................74°
Highest " 12 " M., 30th inst..............................94°

METEOROLOGICAL.

Record of the Thermometer and Rainfall at Braidentown, Florida, for the month of July, 1880, with Remarks in relation to Wind and Weather.

Date.	6 o'clock A. M.	12 o'clock M.	6 o'clock P. M.	Wind at M.	Rainfall.	Remarks.
1	82	96	82	S. W.	1¾ in.	Rain during the afternoon.
2	82	92	87	S. W.	¼ in.	" " "
3	84	91	90	S. W.	......	Clear.
4	84	91	84	S. W.	......	Cloudy.
5	82	93	91	S. W.	......	Clear.
6	84	92	88	S. W.	......	Scotch mist in the afternoon.
7	84	79	84	S. E.	1/16 in.	Rain during P. M.
8	84	93	89	S. E.	½ in.	" " "
9	81	85	81	S. E.	¾ in.	" " "
10	82	92	88	S. W.	......	Clear.
11	86	89	82	S. W.	......	Cloudy, with Scotch mist.
12	82	84	86	S. W.	......	" " "
13	83	93	87	S. W.	......	Cloudy.
14	86	90	83	S. W.	½ in.	Rain in the afternoon.
15	82	92	88	S. W	......	Cloudy.
16	88	90	88	S. W.	......	"
17	86	89	88	S. E.	......	"
18	84	93	90	S. W.	......	"
19	86	90	88	S. W.	......	"
20	88	91	89	S. W.	......	Clear.
21	88	93	90	S. W.	......	"
22	88	90	87	S. W.	¼ in.	Cloudy; rain in the evening.
23	84	92	84	S. W.	......	Cloudy.
24	84	93	88	S. W.	1½ in.	Cloudy; rain in the evening.
25	84	94	82	S. E.	......	Scotch mist in the afternoon.
26	80	80	83	S. E.	½ in.	Rain in the evening.
27	80	80	83	S. E.	1 in.	" " afternoon.
28	80	87	83	S. E.	⅛ in.	" " "
29	83	90	87	S. W.	......	Cloudy and misty.
30	82	90	85	S. W.	......	Clear.
31	80	84	83	S. W.	1/10 in.	Rain at noon.
Sums,	2,593	2,778	2,688	......	7¼ in.	
Av'ge	83¾	89½	86¾	......	......	

Lowest temperature at 6 o'clock A. M., 26th, 27th, 28th and 31st insts..80°
Highest " 12 " M., 1st inst.............................. 96°

Notes from Sunland.

METEOROLOGICAL.

Record of the Thermometer and Rainfall at Braidentown, Florida, for the month of August, 1880, with Remarks in relation to Wind and Weather.

Date.	6 o'clock A. M.	12 o'clock M.	6 o'clock P. M.	Wind at M.	Rainfall.	Remarks.
1	82	91	86	S. W.	......	Clear.
2	82	91	83	S. E.	......	"
3	82	90	80	S. W.	1 in.	Rain during night.
4	78	82	79	S. E.	1¼ in.	" " day and night.
5	78	80	82	S. E.	1½ in.	" " forenoon.
6	78	83	82	S. W.	1/10 in.	" " afternoon.
7	79	93	80	S. W.	¼ in.	" " "
8	82	92	84	S. F.	1 in.	" " "
9	82	92	83	S. E.	½ in.	" " "
10	81	91	88	S. E.	......	Cloudy.
11	82	94	80	S. E.	½ in.	Rain in the afternoon.
12	84	94	84	S. E.	½ in.	" " "
13	82	90	87	S. E.	......	Cloudy.
14	81	91	92	S. W.	......	
15	82	93	79	S. E.	½ in	Rain in the afternoon.
16	80	93	84	S. E.	......	Cloudy.
17	82	95	80	S. E.	2 in.	Rain in the afternoon.
18	80	91	86	S. E.	......	Cloudy.
19	78	93	90	S. E.	......	Clear.
20	82	89	86	S. E.	1/16 in.	Cloudy, rain in the P. M.
21	80	89	89	S. W.	......	Clear.
22	84	92	89	S. W.	......	"
23	86	96	90	S. W.	......	"
24	84	93	88	S. E.	1/16 in.	Cloudy, with rain in the P.M.
25	82	95	85	S. W.	¼ in.	" " " " "
26	81	96	88	S. E.	1 in.	" " " " "
27	82	94	91	S. E.	......	Clear.
28	82	95	88	S. E.	......	" [and night.
29	84	84	83	S. W.	3½ in.	Rain, wind blowing gale day
30	78	82	82	S.	3 in.	" " " " "
31	80	90	84	S. E.	1/8 in.	Rain during the forenoon.
Sums,	2,520	2,814	2,642	......	17 in.	
Av'ge	84	93¾	88	......		

Lowest temperature at 6 o'clock A. M., 4th, 5th, 6th, 19th and 30th insts.
78°

Highest   "   12   "   M., 23d and 26th insts.................96°

METEOROLOGICAL.

Record of the Thermometer and Rainfall at Braidentown, Florida, for the month of September, 1880, with Remarks in relation to Wind and Weather.

Date.	6 o'clock A. M.	12 o'clock, M.	6 o'clock P. M.	Wind at M.	Rainfall.	Remarks.
1	81	86	82	S. E.	¼ in.	Cloudy, with rain in P. M.
2	78	88	78	S. W.	1 in.	" " "
3	78	92	81	S.	1 in.	" " "
4	80	92	88	S. E.	......	Clear.
5	82	92	87	S. E.	......	Clear A. M., cloudy P. M.
6	81	90	87	S. E.	......	Clear.
7	81	88	85	S. W.	......	"
8	81	90	84	S. W.	......	"
9	82	92	86	S. W.	½ in.	Rain in the afternoon.
10	80	94	87	S. E.	⅛ in.	" " "
11	82	92	88	S. E.	......	Cloudy.
12	82	94	87	S. W.	1 in.	Rain in the afternoon.
13	80	92	90	S.	½ in.	Clear day, rain during night.
14	82	90	88	S. E.	......	Clear.
15	80	91	83	S. E.	¾ in.	Clear day, rain during night.
16	78	77	78	S. E.	......	Cloudy, with Scotch mist.
17	75	87	88	S. E.	......	Clear.
18	78	85	81	S. E.	......	Cloudy, with strong wind.
19	75	90	81	S. E.	1/16 in.	Clear A. M., rain P. M.
20	78	90	84	S. E.	½ in.	Rain in the afternoon.
21	78	93	88	S. E.	¼ in.	" " "
22	78	92	87	S. E.	......	Clear.
23	78	94	89	S. E.	......	"
24	77	94	90	S. E.	......	"
25	80	90	85	S.	......	"
26	78	92	87	S. W.	¼ in.	Rain during early part of night.
27	80	87	86	S. W.	1 in.	Rain in the morning.
28	85	90	86	N. W.	......	Clear.
29	79	88	84	S. E.	......	"
30	70	90	87	S. E.	......	"
Sums,	2,377	2,702	2,562	......	7⅛ in.	
Av'ge	79¼	90	85	......	......	

Lowest temperature at 6 o'clock A. M., 30th inst............................70°
Highest " 12 " M., 10th, 12th, 23d and 24th insts...94°

METEOROLOGICAL.

Record of the Thermometer and Rainfall at Braidentown, Florida, for the month of October, 1880, with Remarks in relation to Wind and Weather.

Date.	6 o'clock A. M.	12 o'clock M.	6 o'clock P. M.	Wind at M.	Rainfall.	Remarks.
1	73	92	87	S. E.	......	Clear.
2	70	90	85	S. E.	......	"
3	76	92	87	S. E.	......	"
4	76	92	85	S. E.	......	"
5	77	86	81	S. E.	⅛ in.	Cloudy, with rain.
6	76	80	80	S. E.	⅛ in.	" " "
7	78	80	78	S. E.	3 in.	Cloudy, with heavy rain.
8	82	86	85	S. W.	2 in.	Clear A. M., rain P. M.
9	80	82	79	S. E.	......	Cloudy.
10	76	90	87	S.	......	Clear.
11	78	90	86	E.	......	"
12	78	88	82	E.	......	"
13	70	88	88	E.	......	"
14	76	93	82	E.	......	"
15	70	87	82	E.	......	"
16	68	87	80	E.	......	"
17	72	85	77	S.	½ in.	Rain in the afternoon.
18	66	79	75	E.	......	Clear.
19	69	84	81	N. E.	......	"
20	75	86	80	S. E.	⅛ in.	Rain in the morning.
21	70	87	82	S. E.	1 in.	" during the night.
22	78	82	76	N. W.	½ in.	" in the morning.
23	68	78	73	N. W.	......	Clear.
24	62	80	76	S. E.	......	"
25	60	79	80	E.	......	"
26	62	82	80	S. E.	......	"
27	68	86	81	S. E.	......	"
28	74	72	74	S. E.	1¾ in.	Cloudy, with heavy rain.
29	70	80	79	N. W.	¼ in.	" " rain.
30	75	80	76	N. W.	......	Cloudy
31	72	82	78	S. W.	......	Clear.
Sums,	2,245	2,625	2,502	......	9⅜ in.	
Av'ge	72½	84¾	80¾	......		

Lowest temperature at 6 o'clock A. M., 25th inst...........................60°
Highest   "   12   "   M., 14th inst.........................93°

METEOROLOGICAL.

Record of the Thermometer and Rainfall at Braidentown,
Florida, for the month of November, 1880, with Remarks
in relation to Wind and Weather.

Date.	6 o'clock A. M.	12 o'clock M.	6 o'clock P. M.	Wind at M.	Rainfall.	Remarks.
1	68	86	79	S. E.	......	Cloudy A. M., Clear P. M.
2	68	82	78	N. W.	......	Clear A. M., Cloudy P. M.
3	68	83	78	S. W.	......	Clear.
4	70	80	80	N. E.	½ in.	Rain during the night.
5	78	86	82	S.	......	Clear.
6	77	86	81	S.	......	"
7	74	75	76	N.	......	Cloudy.
8	70	80	77	S. E.	......	"
9	72	90	85	E.	......	Clear.
10	77	85	78	S.	......	Cloudy.
11	70	84	78	S. E.	......	Clear.
12	70	82	82	E.	......	"
13	70	87	86	S. E.	......	"
14	74	83	80	S.	¼ in.	Clear day, rain at night.
15	70	70	66	N. E.	......	Cloudy.
16	50	72	71	S. E.	......	Clear.
17	60	75	73	W.	......	"
18	64	80	76	W.	. ....	Cloudy.
19	70	78	79	E.	......	"
20	77	75	72	N. E.	½ in.	Rain in the forenoon.
21	62	76	77	E.	......	Clear A. M., Cloudy P. M.
22	68	84	76	E.	......	" " " "
23	63	76	67	N. E.	......	Cloudy.
24	65	79	79	S. E.	......	"
25	71	80	74	N. W.	......	" and foggy.
26	71	75	75	S. E.	......	"
27	72	80	76	S. E.	......	Clear.
28	71	84	78	S.	......	"
29	71	84	84	S. E.	......	"
30	70	86	78	S. E.	......	"
Sums.	2,081	2,412	2,321	......	1¼ in.	
Av'ge	69⅓	80⅓	77⅓	......	......	

Lowest temperature at 6 o'clock A. M., 16th inst...........................50°
Highest " 12 " M., 9th inst........................90°

METEOROLOGICAL.

Record of the Thermometer and Rainfall at Braidentown, Florida, for the month of December, 1880, with Remarks in relation to Wind and Weather.

Date.	6 o'clock A. M.	12 o'clock M.	6 o'clock P. M.	Wind at M.	Rainfall.	Remarks.
1	71	80	80	S.	......	Cloudy.
2	76	84	84	W.	......	"
3	72	82	82	S. W.	......	Clear.
4	69	82	80	S.	......	"
5	70	82	78	S.	......	"
6	76	77	73	S. W.	¼ in.	Cloudy, with rain.
7	56	68	65	N. E.	......	Clear.
8	45	72	64	E.	......	"
9	52	73	72	N. E.	......	"
10	52	69	68	N. E.	......	"
11	45	72	69	N. E.	......	"
12	50	75	72	N. E.	......	"
13	50	79	75	N. W.	......	"
14	58	78	70	S. E.	......	"
15	60	78	73	S.	......	"
16	65	81	75	S.	......	"
17	66	82	75	S.	......	"
18	70	82	74	S. W.	¾ in.	Rain morning and afternoon.
19	70	77	70	S.	½ in.	Rain in the afternoon.
20	70	81	65	N. W.	......	Cloudy.
21	58	60	55	N. W.	......	"
22	42	56	54	N. E.	......	"
23	46	71	68	S. E.	......	Clear.
24	58	71	67	S. W.	......	"
25	62	69	68	S.	⅛ in.	Rain in the afternoon.
26	52	66	58	N. E.	......	Cloudy.
27	52	63	60	N. W.	......	"
28	43	65	65	S. E.	......	Clear.
29	54	71	60	S. E.	⅛ in.	Rain in the afternoon.
30	40	51	45	N. W.	......	Cloudy. [of the year.
31	38	50	53	N. E.	1 in.	Drizzling rain. Coldest day
Sums,	1,788	2,237	2,117	......	2¾ in.	
Av'ge	57¾	74⅓	68¼	......	......	

Lowest temperature at 6 o'clock A. M., 31st inst.............................38°
Highest   "   12   "   M., 2d inst...............................84°

METEOROLOGICAL.

Record of the Thermometer and Rainfall at Braidentown, Florida, for the month of January, 1881, with Remarks in relation to Wind and Weather.

Date.	6 o'clock A. M.	12 o'clock M.	6 o'clock P. M.	Wind at M.	Rainfall.	Remarks.
1	54	78	59	S.	1½ in.	Rain during the afternoon.
2	50	67	63	E.	......	Clear.
3	46	74	70	E.	......	"
4	69	80	77	S.	......	"
5	74	79	71	S.	1 in.	Rain nearly all day.
6	66	68	66	E.	⅛ in.	Rain in the afternoon.
7	63	67	67	E.	1 in.	Rain morning and afternoon.
8	65	68	69	S. E.	½ in.	Rain in the afternoon.
9	66	75	72	S. E.	......	Cloudy.
10	73	80	75	S.	¼ in.	Rain during the night.
11	68	76	65	N. W.	⅛ in.	" afternoon.
12	54	62	62	E.	......	Cloudy.
13	48	78	75	E.	......	Clear.
14	64	75	70	S.	......	Cloudy.
15	68	77	70	W.	⅛ in.	Rain in the afternoon.
16	66	82	76	S. W.	......	Clear.
17	64	83	80	S. E.	......	"
18	66	87	79	E.	......	"
19	66	83	78	S. E.	......	"
20	66	77	72	S.	......	Cloudy, with Scotch mist.
21	66	75	70	S. W.	......	Clear A. M., cloudy P. M.
22	60	76	66	S. E.	......	Clear.
23	57	60	58	N. E.	¼ in.	Rain P. M. and night.
24	53	60	56	N. W.	¼ in.	" "
25	52	55	52	N. E.	......	Cloudy.
26	44	76	64	N. E.	......	Clear.
27	48	72	62	N. E.	......	"
28	54	67	64	N. E.	......	Cloudy.
29	56	80	74	E.	......	Clear.
30	60	78	76	N. W.	......	"
31	55	78	74	N. W.	......	"
Sums.	1,861	2,293	2,132	......	5⅛ in.	
Av'ge	60	74	68¾	......	......	

Lowest temperature at 6 o'clock A. M., 26th inst.............................44°
Highest   "   12   "   M., 17th and 19th insts................83°

METEOROLOGICAL.

Record of the Thermometer and Rainfall at Braidèntown, Florida, for the month of February, 1881, with Remarks in relation to Wind and Weather.

Date.	6 o'clock A. M.	12 o'clock M.	6 o'clock P. M.	Wind at M.	Rainfall.	Remarks.
1	56	76	72	S. E.	......	Clear.
2	65	71	70	S. W.	¼ in.	Rain in the afternoon.
3	54	70	67	S. W.	......	Clear.
4	50	65	62	S. E.	......	Cloudy.
5	52	75	69	N. E.	......	Clear.
6	62	75	69	N. E.	......	Clear, wind blowing a gale.
7	66	78	72	N. E.	......	" " " "
8	64	79	73	E.	......	" " " "
9	68	72	70	S. E.	⅛ in.	Rain in the afternoon.
10	65	84	78	S. E.	......	Clear.
11	70	81	75	S.	......	"
12	64	72	64	S. W.	⅛ in.	Rain in the afternoon.
13	66	69	59	W.	......	Clear.
14	48	66	62	N. W.	......	"
15	52	75	66	N. W.	......	"
16	58	80	74	N. E.	......	"
17	59	84	76	S. E.	......	"
18	62	85	76	S. E.	......	"
19	67	82	74	S. E.	......	"
20	69	81	74	S. W.	......	"
21	65	76	69	N. W.	......	"
22	60	80	66	S. W.	......	"
23	58	80	73	S. E.	......	"
24	58	80	74	N. E.	......	"
25	60	79	74	E.	......	Cloudy.
26	60	84	77	S. E.	......	Clear. [gale.
27	65	79	69	S.	2 in.	Rain, with wind blowing a
28	69	76	66	W.	......	Clear, " " "
Sums,	1,712	2,054	1,970	......	2½ in.	
Av'ge	61⅞	73½	70½	......	......	

Lowest temperature at 6 o'clock A. M., 14th inst......................................48°
Highest   "   12   "   M., 18th inst......................................85°

METEOROLOGICAL.

Record of the Thermometer and Rainfall at Braidentown, Florida, for the month of March, 1881, with Remarks in relation to Wind and Weather.

Date.	6 o'clock A. M.	12 o'clock M.	6 o'clock P. M.	Wind at M.	Rainfall.	Remarks.
1	59	74	61	N. W.	......	Clear.
2	59	75	69	N. W.	......	"
3	62	75	71	S. W.	......	"
4	59	71	63	N. W.	......	"
5	66	74	63	N. W.	......	"
6	59	68	68	N. W.	......	"
7	53	72	73	E.	......	"
8	60	78	69	S.	1¼ in.	Rain P. M. and night.
9	62	78	67	N. W.	......	Clear.
10	57	72	70	S. E.	......	"
11	52	79	73	S. E.	......	"
12	73	81	75	S. W.	......	Cloudy, with Scotch mist.
13	73	75	72	N. W.	......	" " "
14	65	80	77	N. E.	......	Cloudy.
15	67	88	80	N. E.	......	Clear.
16	67	83	75	S.	......	"
17	66	80	76	S. W.	......	"
18	72	82	78	S. W.	......	"
19	72	79	76	S. W.	1 in.	Cloudy, rain P.M. and night.
20	68	70	64	N. W.	......	Cloudy.
21	63	74	67	S. W.	¼ in.	Cloudy, with rain at night.
22	62	65	61	N. E	......	Clear, wind blowing a gale.
23	52	66	58	N. W.	......	Clear.
24	59	74	71	N. W.	......	"
25	56	74	66	S. W.	......	"
26	65	70	69	S. W.	......	Cloudy.
27	60	72	63	S. W.	......	Clear.
28	52	78	71	S. E.	......	"
29	57	75	70	S. W.	......	"
30	59	65	64	N. W.	......	Clear, wind blowing a gale.
31	60	68	63	N. W.	......	" " "
Sums,	1,914	2,315	2,143	......	2½ in.	
Av'ge	62	74¾	69½	......		

Lowest temperature at 6 o'clock, A. M., 11th, 23d and 28th insts.....52°
Highest   "   12   "   M., 15th inst............................80°

www.ingramcontent.com/pod-product-compliance
Lightning Source LLC
Chambersburg PA
CBHW021427090426
42742CB00009B/1295